W9-DFD-317

# BERTOLT BRECHT

# Mother Courage and Her Children

*Translated by*
JOHN WILLETT

*Edited with an Introduction by*
JOHN WILLETT *and* RALPH MANHEIM

*Introduction to the Penguin Classics Edition by*
NORMAN ROESSLER

*Foreword by*
OLYMPIA DUKAKIS

PENGUIN BOOKS

PENGUIN BOOKS
Published by the Penguin Group
Penguin Group (USA) Inc., 375 Hudson Street, New York, New York 10014, U.S.A.
Penguin Group (Canada), 90 Eglinton Avenue East, Suite 700, Toronto,
Ontario, Canada M4P 2Y3 (a division of Pearson Penguin Canada Inc.)
Penguin Books Ltd, 80 Strand, London WC2R 0RL, England
Penguin Ireland, 25 St Stephen's Green, Dublin 2, Ireland (a division of Penguin Books Ltd)
Penguin Group (Australia), 250 Camberwell Road, Camberwell, Victoria 3124,
Australia (a division of Pearson Australia Group Pty Ltd)
Penguin Books India Pvt Ltd, 11 Community Centre, Panchsheel Park, New Delhi – 110 017, India
Penguin Group (NZ), 67 Apollo Drive, Rosedale, North Shore 0632,
New Zealand (a division of Pearson New Zealand Ltd)
Penguin Books (South Africa) (Pty) Ltd, 24 Sturdee Avenue,
Rosebank, Johannesburg 2196, South Africa

Penguin Books Ltd, Registered Offices:
80 Strand, London WC2R 0RL, England

First published in Great Britain by Eyre Methuen Ltd. 1980
First published in the United States of America by Arcade Publishing, Inc. 1994
Published by arrangement with Arcade Publishing, Inc.
This edition with a foreword by Olympia Dukakis and introductions by
Norman Roessler published in Penguin Books 2007

1  3  5  7  9  10  8  6  4  2

Copyright © Arvid Englind Teaterforlag, a.b., 1940
Copyright renewed Stefan S. Brecht, 1967
Copyright © Suhrkamp Verlag, Frankfurt am Main, 1949
Translation for play and texts by Brecht copyright © Stefan S. Brecht, 1980
Introduction by Ralph Manheim and John Willett and editorial notes copyright © Eyre Methuen Ltd., 1980
Foreword copyright © Olympia Dukakis, 2007
Introductions copyright © Norman Roessler, 2007
All rights reserved

*Mother Courage and Her Children*, originally published in German under the title
*Mutter Courage und ihre Kinder,* was first published in this translation in 1980.

CAUTION: This play is fully protected by copyright. All inquiries concerning the rights for professional or amateur stage production and concerning the music for this play should be directed to Jerold L. Couture, Fitelson, Lasky, Aslan & Couture, 551 Fifth Avenue, New York, New York 10176. Outside the United States of America, inquiries concerning the rights for professional stage production and concerning the music for this play should be directed to the International Copyright Bureau Ltd., 22a Aubrey House, Maida Avenue, London W2 1TQ, England, and those for amateur stage production to Samuel French Ltd., 52 Fitzroy Street, London W1T 5JR, England. Inquiries about use of any material other than in performance should be directed to Arcade Publishing, Inc., 116 John Street, New York, New York 10038.

LIBRARY OF CONGRESS CATALOGING IN PUBLICATION DATA
Brecht, Bertolt, 1898–1956.
[Mutter Courage und ihre Kinder. English]
Mother Courage and her children / Bertolt Brecht; translated by John Willett; edited with an introduction
by John Willett and Ralph Manheim; introduction to the Penguin Classics Edition by Norman Roessler;
foreword by Olympia Dukakis.
p. cm.
Includes bibliographical references.
ISBN 978-0-14-310528-2
1. Thirty Years' War, 1618–1648—Drama. I. Willett, John. II. Manheim, Ralph, 1907– III. Title.
PT2603.R397M82 2008
832'.912—dc22     2007037257

Printed in the United States of America
Set in Adobe Sabon

Except in the United States of America, this book is sold subject to the condition that it shall not, by way of trade or otherwise, be lent, resold, hired out, or otherwise circulated without the publisher's prior consent in any form of binding or cover other than that in which it is published and without a similar condition including this condition being imposed on the subsequent purchaser.

The scanning, uploading and distribution of this book via the Internet or via any other means without the permission of the publisher is illegal and punishable by law. Please purchase only authorized electronic editions, and do not participate in or encourage electronic piracy of copyrighted materials. Your support of the author's rights is appreciated.

PENGUIN

# MOTHER COURAGE AND HER CHILDREN

BERTOLT BRECHT was born in Augsburg, Bavaria, in 1898 and left Germany in 1933 when Hitler came to power. He lived in the United States for seven years, settling with his family in Santa Monica and New York, and continued to work on plays and films. After the war, Brecht returned to Germany, where he founded the Berliner Ensemble. He died in 1956.

OLYMPIA DUKAKIS has worked for more than forty years as an actress, director, producer, teacher, and activist. She received the Academy Award, the New York Film Critics Award, the Los Angeles Film Critics Award, and the Golden Globe Award for her work in the film *Moonstruck*. She has also received two OBIE Awards, including one for her work in Bertolt Brecht's *A Man's a Man*. In 2003, Dukakis published her national best-selling autobiography *Ask Me Again Tomorrow: A Life in Progress*. She has appeared in more than 130 theatrical productions. Dukakis lives in New York City.

NORMAN ROESSLER, PhD, is editor of *Communications*, the performance journal of the International Brecht Society, and is a lecturer at Temple University in Philadelphia, Pennsylvania.

# Contents

# Foreword

Throughout my career as an actor, I performed as Mother Courage in four productions: in the 1960s at the Charles Playhouse in Boston, in the 1970s at the Whole Theatre in Montclair, New Jersey, and in the 1990s at Williamstown Theatre in Massachusetts and the Cleveland Public Theatre in Ohio. Brecht is one of my favorite playwrights, along with Chekhov, Turgenev, Williams, Racine, and O'Neill.

Certain elements of Brecht's writing and stage productions challenge an actor. Although there are longer scenes in *Life of Galileo* and *The Good Person of Szechwan*, the short duration of scenes in *Mother Courage* demands precise, uncluttered, and singular statements of character and intent. The arc of the character developmental line is truncated because of the brevity of the scenes, which forces you to present the character as full-bodied at the beginning of a scene. In other words, there is no easing into it as an actor. There is no time for big speeches, and the plot moves along quickly.

In 1989, I traveled to East Germany for the premiere of *Steel Magnolias*, which was the first Western film to be shown in East Germany after the Berlin Wall came down. During my trip, I visited the Berliner Ensemble at the Theater am Schiffbauerdamm, a modest-sized theatre where Brecht produced his shows. I was surprised by the size of the theatre. In the United States we tend to produce Brecht on large stages, which I think demonstrates our misunderstanding of what an "epic" is: we, as "westerners," think of a large space rather than a larger historical vista. I realized that the intimacy of the Berliner Ensemble theatre made the comedy so much easier to achieve, and the more dramatic moments less theatricalized.

At present, I am working on the Greek tragedies and Brecht and reading *Euripides and the Instruction of the Athenians* by Justina Gregory. I feel that there is a connection between Brecht's plays and those of Euripides—*Trojan Women, Hecuba, Heracles*—and other Greek dramatists. In the Greek tragedies and in *Mother Courage*—and in Brecht's *The Resistible Rise of Arturo Ui* and *A Man's a Man*—we witness a blindness to why war is waged. Indeed, war may even provide a purpose for living. Chris Hedges's recent book *War Is a Force That Gives Us Meaning*, which goes back to *The Iliad*, helps us understand that this is a timeless dilemma. Plato said, "Only the dead have seen the end of war." This endlessness is felt in *Mother Courage*, which is set during the Thirty Years War, and in *Hecuba*, during the Trojan War. The children of both Courage and Hecuba are killed during the wars, but both women want to triumph in war. Some scholars believe the Trojan War was really about the Greeks controlling trade routes and the sea lanes, couched in the language of honor and pride, much as the George W. Bush administration couched its efforts to control oil in the language of upholding democracy. For Courage, the war is openly about profit. We see what is happening to Courage's humanity; she does not register the price she pays to succeed. Her efforts to win at business conflict with a mother's need to protect her children. Since acting roles central to this kind of conflict are usually male, playing the role of Courage is particularly unique and challenging for me.

The Greeks and Brecht are intentionally instructional. They mean to show us how *not* to live, in order to show us how to organize our life and society through certain values. For the Greeks, everything depended on persuasion; they made arguments in order to penetrate to the heart of an issue and convince their audience to adopt a specific idea or point of view. Brecht is the same; he is about the argument. Brecht asks his viewers to have feelings about specific things; in this he avoids indulging in what we think of today as subjective internalized landscapes. Like the Greeks, Brecht wants to manipulate his audience to think in a way that he himself values, and to be moved by those things he, as the playwright, finds important. In *Mother Courage*, Brecht exposes war as nothing but big business and the acquisition of natural resources and territory. He illustrates the dehumanization of business, of war and politics. Brecht presents a story of classical hubris and reveals how capitalism breeds greed, injustice, and privilege. He wants us to say no to capitalism and yes to socialism. The Greeks wrote about the politics of justice, and how the laws are manipulated by the elite.

Everything in the original production of *Mother Courage* was specifically detailed and chronicled by Brecht, including the dimensions of the wagon. In the Williamstown and Cleveland productions that I participated in, the set designer Doug Stein built the wagon to Brecht's specifications. I remember the day they pulled the wagon—to much fanfare—from the workshop through the streets of Williamstown, Massachusetts. It was surprisingly light to pull around on stage.

One of the most memorable scenes in *Mother Courage* for me is one in which—in the Williamstown production—my own daughter, Christina, played the role of Courage's daughter, Kattrin. Women are at the heart of the major issues in *Mother Courage*. In the play, Kattrin is mute, implying that she has been the victim of sexual abuse by one of the soldiers. There is a town full of children that the army is preparing to attack. Kattrin determines to sound off the alarm by beating on a drum from a rooftop to alert the town of the danger. While Courage's single-minded need is to prevail during the war, Kattrin's need is to save the children. Brecht illuminates through Courage's children different paths of survival or suffering during war: the exploitation of patriotism, in Eilif, the oldest son who joins the army; loyalty, in the younger son, Swiss Cheese; and empathy, in her daughter, Kattrin. In Kattrin, we see how compassion and tenderness are always in danger. Brecht's message is: how can we call ourselves human if there is no compassion or empathy?

Courage believes she is a winner—she thinks she's going to make it and that her business will flourish. She starts and ends the play the same way ("Wait for me") because she thinks she is still in the game of the business of war. But in reality, Courage ends up yoked to her wagon like an animal. This wagon that she thought would allow her to win causes her destruction, but she does not acknowledge this.

In the end, the audience is painfully moved by her tenacity and her willingness to go forth. That Courage refuses to change is where our recognition lies. Even as the audience is appalled at the price she has paid, at her blindness and her unquestioning acceptance of the status quo, her story reflects the complexities and compromises we must deal with in real life to survive. Critics and scholars say Brecht did not want the audience to be moved by her, but in her we see ourselves, our own dilemmas and contradictions, and at the same time admire this deep urge to go forth. Even if a production of this play does not work, that last moment, that great moment, is almost impossible to destroy.

—OLYMPIA DUKAKIS

# Introduction to the Penguin Classics Edition

## BERTOLT BRECHT

*First comes eating and then comes morality.*

*Staring is not seeing.*

*Thinking is one of the chief pleasures of the human race.*

Whether reading or viewing the work of the German artist Bertolt Brecht (1898–1956), one is greeted by a series of titles, gestures, images, aphorisms—like those listed above and below—which may be written on placards lowered from the rafters, projected on film screens, expressed through the performative body, or delivered with a hammerlike thud on the written page. On a linguistic, aesthetic, and philosophical level these effects are meant to pull the reader out of a passive and unconscious state of mind and into a condition of heightened awareness that leads to an alternative way of thinking and acting in the world. Such devices were just one element of Brecht's notion of a "dialectical theatre"—a performance experience that explored, examined, and challenged traditional ideas of Western aesthetic philosophy as well as confronted the most important political and historical issues of the day in an intensely intellectual, oftentimes contradictory, yet always pleasurable manner.

*To be good, yet live.*

*War teaches people nothing.*

*Whoever empathizes with someone, and does so completely, relinquishes criticism both of the object of their empathy and of*

*themselves. Instead of awakening, they sleepwalk. Instead of do-*
*ing something, they let something be done with them.*

At the dawn of the twenty-first century, as the terrible
landmarks of the previous century (the Holocaust, the World
Wars, the nuclear age) lose their immediacy and power and
the new century brings new monuments to our world (9/11, eth-
nic cleansing, global warming), we find Brecht—who seemed so
absolutely determined by the twentieth century and hence rendered null and void by its end—to be even more relevant. For
Brecht, although a product of the "dark times" of the twentieth
century, nevertheless was not imprisoned by the era that he lived
in. Brecht mediated his times through the grander lens of Western history, philosophy, and aesthetics; hence Brecht provides
not just a conversation with the twentieth century but a dialogue which reaches back through Nietzsche, Ibsen, Marx,
Shakespeare, Aristotle, Sophocles, and Socrates and forward to
our current postmodern epoch. Moreover, it is not a simple conversation Brecht provides, but rather an elegant puzzle that includes the constant sting of the irritating Socratic gadfly. At
every moment that we experience theatre, film, music, art, or
video games, we feel the jab of Brecht asking us to stay awake,
retain our critical faculties, conceive our existence in an aesthetic way, and finally intervene and change the world that we
have constructed—because our life depends on it.

*The proof of the pudding lies in the eating.*

*The philosophers have in various ways only interpreted the*
*world; the point, however, is to change it.* (Karl Marx)

## ORIGINS

*I have always needed the spur of contradiction.*

Brecht was born in Augsburg, Germany (in southwestern Germany, near Munich) in 1898 to comfortable middle-class par-

ents, and he enjoyed a fairly normal childhood. Often sickly, and an inattentive student at school, he found early inspiration in the work of writers such as Villon, Rimbaud, and Wedekind, and as a result produced a number of poems, songs, and play fragments throughout his youth. One of his earliest school friends from this period, Caspar Neher, would later design many of the stages for Brecht's theatrical work. Neither military service (as a medical orderly) at the end of World War I nor university education (one semester) at the University of Munich decisively affected his life, but in the same year, 1918, he did finish his first play, *Baal*. Until 1924 he would be based largely in Munich (with several important trips to Berlin); it was a period in which he would establish important relationships with Herbert Ihering (Berlin theatre critic) and Helene Weigel (Jewish-Austrian Marxist actor and future wife) and write plays that would define his early career—*Drums in the Night* (1919), *In the Jungle of the Cities* (1922)—as well as work with the material that would become *A Man's a Man* (1926). *Drums in the Night* would be his first play to be produced on the stage, in September 1922 at the Munich Kammerspiele; when it premiered in Berlin in December of the same year it proved to be a decisive impetus for his career.

Brecht moved to Berlin in 1924, where he would be based until 1933, and as the Golden Age of the Weimar Republic played out, he would elevate his career to an international level. The Weimar Republic (equivalent to the Roaring Twenties in America) was the collective name given to the political society of Germany between the end of World War I (1918) and the rise of Adolf Hitler (1933). Similar to the French Revolution of the eighteenth century, the Weimar Republic is both a primer and cautionary tale about a Western, democratic, and capitalist culture that extends itself too far and descends into decadence, chaos, hyperinflation, and ultimately totalitarian dictatorship. It was during this period that Brecht established a collaborative relationship with both Elisabeth Hauptmann and Kurt Weill, worked with two famous directors (Max Reinhardt at the Deutsches Theater and Erwin Piscator at his Dramaturgical Collective), turned intellectually and politically to Marxism, and published a groundbreaking book of poems, *Hauspostille* (*Domestic Breviary*). *The Threepenny Opera* premiered in August 1928 at the Theater am Schiffbauerdamm in Berlin, which would later become the home theatre of Brecht's theatre collective, the Berliner Ensemble (BE), after World War II. The premiere was a huge success, catapulting Brecht and Weill to national and international fame.

The *Threepenny Opera* moment is often seen as both the high point and fall of the Weimar Republic. With the onset of the Great Depression in October 1929, the Weimar Republic quickly descended into political and cultural chaos, which would eventually see the rise of Hitler and the Nazi Party. In these last years of the Weimar Republic, Brecht would continue his collaborative work with Hauptmann and Weill, establish new collaborative relationships with Margarete Steffin, Hanns Eisler, and Slatan Dudow, which would produce works such as the opera *Rise and Fall of the City of Mahagonny*, the film *Kuhle Wampe*, and didactic plays such as *The Measures Taken*. Hitler became chancellor on January 30, 1933, and consolidated power through numerous acts of political terror and propaganda. Brecht, as the writer of *The Threepenny Opera* and with announced Marxist leanings, was on the short list of Nazi enemies, and hence, a day after the Reichstag fire, wasted no time fleeing into exile.

In exile, Brecht took up residence in various countries: Denmark, 1933–1939; Sweden, 1939–1940; Finland, 1940–1941; and the United States, 1941–1947. Operating without a native language, stage, culture, or audience, Brecht nevertheless was able to produce theoretical, theatrical, and poetic work that has come to define his later career. In Denmark he established a collaborative relationship with Ruth Berlau, thus completing (along with Helene Weigel, Elisabeth Hauptmann, and Margarete Steffin) what contemporary scholarship, based on John Fuegi's 1994 book *Brecht & Co.: Sex, Politics, and the Making of the Modern Drama*, has come to understand as Brecht's inner circle. This inner circle has been defined in various ways: at its best, as a free, fluid, and equal collaborative ensemble that accepted the single designation of "Brecht" for collaborative work; at its worst, as an exploitative/parasitic relationship in which Brecht, through sex and charisma, rendered invisible the authorship and voice of his female collaborators.

This conundrum brings up the issue of authorship—whether the work of art is ever just the effort of one person, or whether single authorship ultimately is based on the necessity of granting authorship to one individual instead of a group. Brecht is an extreme version of this problem, because his aesthetic works are monuments to fluidity—constantly being written and rewritten and hence never stable.

Beginning in 1938–1939 (a period that encompassed the onset of the Holocaust, prefigured through Kristallnacht on November 9, 1938, and the beginning of World War II with the invasion of Poland on September 1, 1939), Brecht would produce his great, mature works: *Life of Galileo, The Good Person of Szechwan, Mother Courage and Her Children, The Messingkauf Dialogues, The Resistible Rise of Arturo Ui,* and *The Caucasian Chalk Circle.* After the end of World War II in 1945 he stayed in the United States for an additional two years waiting to see what would happen in Germany and whether he could make it in the American theatre and film industry. In October 1947, he was called to testify before the U.S. House Un-American Activities Committee (HUAC), which was investigating communist and anti-American activity. To the dismay of many, he did not invoke his right not to testify, and instead performed an ambivalent piece of political theatre, which in the end left everyone confused. This was his swan song in America, and he embarked the following day for Switzerland.

With the successful premiere of *Mother Courage* (with Helene Weigel assaying the title role) at the Deutsches Theatre in Berlin, as well as the publication of *A Short Organum for the Theatre* (a distillation of *The Messingkauf Dialogues*) in January 1949, Brecht successfully reintroduced himself to the European theatre scene. Germany was now a divided country, the concrete and symbolic center of the Cold War conflict between the United States and the Soviet Union, a situation which would last until 1990 when Germany was reunified. Brecht settled in East Berlin (yet kept his Austrian passport and Swiss bank accounts), eventually founding, along with Helene Weigel, the Berliner Ensemble in 1949. In the last years of his life he worked to bring all his theatrical work to the postwar audience and at the same time attempted to negotiate the ambivalences of the Cold War. Beginning in 1954, the BE undertook a series of guest residencies throughout Europe, and it was largely through these tours which thrust the BE and Brecht's theatrical work back into the international scene. He died in August 1956.

Over the last fifty years, Brecht has continued to play the Socratic gadfly, fascinating and irritating us at the same time. The aesthetic philosophy of Brecht comprises a number of challenging terms (ranging from *alienation effects* to *social gestus* to *epic theatre* to *non–Aristotelian Theatre*) but for the sake of simplicity and convenience this edition utilizes the summary term *Dialectical Theatre*, which Brecht himself favored at the end of his life. In short, Dialectical Theatre resists absolutes, essentials, and identifications and instead seeks out contradictions, diversities, and multiplicities. Nothing is eternal, all is fluid, and so, ultimately, all is changeable. In Dialectical Theatre, the writer, actor, and spectator are consciously and cognitively involved in the performance they are collectively creating. This position stands in contrast to the main tradition of Western performance—what Brecht referred to as the Aristotelian tradition—in which one is asked to identify, empathize, and lose oneself to the illusion and mystery of the performance.

In his theatrical works, but especially his theoretical writings, Brecht explored this idea of Dialectical Theatre. Indeed, what distinguishes Brecht most is his philosophical-theoretical work, which accompanies his performance work. Brecht left behind extensive aesthetic writings, contained in seven volumes in the standard edition of his complete works in German, yet these writings do not form a systematic or even consistent expression of an aesthetic theory. What Brecht gives us in his writings are political and aesthetic puzzles, meant to stimulate awareness and critical thinking, which Brecht believed were necessary and pleasurable endeavors within the human condition.

# THE PROOF OF THE PUDDING:
# READING BRECHT

"The proof of the pudding lies in the eating" was a favored motto of Brecht's and constantly reminded him that performance was about actions and not about theories. In this introduction, much has been said about Brecht's art, but how does all this theoretical commentary translate into actually reading Brecht? The text, as a work of art, is never a destination, but a portal experience. This is especially true of the performance text, and above all true of the Brechtian performance text. Here are some of the portals that the reader should consider when reading these editions of Brecht in translation: (1) the primary play script and its variations; (2) the secondary material that accompanies the play script (theoretical ruminations, dramaturgical explanations, and photo descriptions); (3) the musical "text" contained within the play script—songs, compositions; (4) extension of the play script into other genres—theoretical essay, novel, film adaptation; (5) the significant global theatrical productions over the last fifty years; and (6) the translations and adaptations into different languages.

When reading Brecht, one should keep these portals in mind as accompaniment in the reading of the primary text. For example, when reading the primary play script, one should not be afraid to use the secondary material located in the back of the text as part of the performance material. Stopping one's reading in mid-piece to consult another text is Brechtian in itself, and perusing the theoretical material and the questions and contradictions that they bring up will expand the puzzle of the text. Also, keep in mind that the Willett/Manheim translations used in this edition are not the only translations, and others from Eric Bentley, Tony Kushner, and David Hare (to name just a few) will show different ways of rendering the text. The image, or the description of the image, from a historical production (e.g., Helene Weigel's "silent scream" in *Mother Courage*, Martin Wuttke contorting himself into a human swastika in *Arturo Ui*), and the sound of a song in variation renditions (e.g.,

"Mack the Knife" from *The Threepenny Opera* sung by Kurt Gerron, Bertolt Brecht, Scott Merrill, Bobby Darin, Sting, or Cyndi Lauper, or the "Alabama Song" from *Mahagonny* sung by Lotte Lenya, Jim Morrison, and Marilyn Manson) are all methods of constructing a richer experience.

# MOTHER COURAGE
# AND HER CHILDREN


## WAR TEACHES PEOPLE NOTHING

"Relentless," describes the mechanisms of war, but it is equally valid as a description of Brecht's *Mother Courage and Her Children*, for perhaps no other literary or performative work has so relentlessly and ruthlessly engaged in such a critical-aesthetic experiment on war. When we read *Mother Courage* we see the cultural memory of war (the Thirty Years War, World War II, Vietnam War, Bosnia, War on Terrorism) as well as the aesthetic memory of war (*Iliad, Antigone, Simplicissimus, Guernica, Henry IV, All Quiet on the Western Front, The Deerhunter, Jarhead*) and the pop cultural discourse on war (*Terminator, Matrix*), but with one major difference: Brecht consistently blocks the reader's path to catharsis, redemption, or pornographic ecstasy. "War teaches people nothing," Brecht intones in a 1954 fragment on *Mother Courage*, and this is the aesthetic and critical enterprise that he pursues throughout the play script and the additional secondary material. Brecht wants to deconstruct war so that it has no meaning or learning curve. War, whether conceived as heroic violence or suffering, unavoidable necessity, or noble if tragic endeavor, does not, according to Brecht, teach us any deeper truth about our natures, our behaviors, or our capacities. The idea that war is eternal, unavoidable, heroic, economic—and therefore ultimately meaningful—is the most pernicious illusion or drug that we can submit ourselves to. This goes not only for those who validate war but for those who oppose it. To believe that antiwar ideas can be derived from stories or depictions of war is the ultimate illusion in the Western imagination. Brecht understood, well before Anthony Swofford in his 2003 Gulf War I chronicle *Jarhead*, that all performative discourse on war, even the most antiwar, never rises above "pornography"—hence the dangerous high-wire act Brecht performs with *Mother Courage* and its setting within the Thirty Years War.

## STORY

For such a relentless and ruthlessly intellectual and emotional piece, it is a stunningly simple story. Anna Fierling, aka Mother Courage, a canteen woman during the Thirty Years War (1618–1648) that decimated much of Central Europe, especially Germany, struggles to keep herself, her canteen business (contained in a wagon), and her three children alive during the middle phase of the war. Fought sporadically over three decades, with various national and religious combatants, it was a harbinger of the world wars that would decimate the twentieth century in Brecht's lifetime. Mother Courage wants to survive the war, but she also needs the war—because war is "business by other means"—and so she must balance survival and profit throughout. At the end of the play, she has achieved only one of these—her own survival. All three children are dead, all her comrades are gone, yet she still has the animal instinct to hitch herself to her decrepit canteen wagon, and chase the army caravan.

## ORIGINS

Brecht wrote the play over the course of five weeks (September 27–November 3, 1939) while in exile in Sweden. The immediate impetus for the play was the Nazi invasion of Poland on September 1, 1939, which initiated World War II. However, it appears that Brecht had been mulling over the basic material and theatrical presentation for at least a year beforehand. This would place the original kernel of the work in the last year of his Danish exile, an important transition point in his career. After working on two plays with contemporary relevance and a more realistic aesthetic (*Señora Carrar's Rifles*, about the Spanish Civil War, and *Fear and Misery in the Third Reich*), Brecht turned to more distant historical subject matter and Dialectical Theatre aesthetic, which would produce works such as *Galileo, The Messingkauf Dialogues*, and *The Good Person of Szechwan*.

Brecht met the Swedish actress Naima Wifstrand in the summer of 1939 and learned the story of Lotte Svärd, a fictional canteen woman in *Tales of the Subaltern* (1848), written by the Swedish writer Johan Ludvig Runeberg. Initially, the story seemed to offer Brecht a chance to gain entree to the Swedish stage, with Wifstrand's presence as the lead actor. (What would later become the part of mute Kattrin was originally assigned to Brecht's wife, Helene Weigel, to allow her to return to the stage, even though she spoke no Swedish.) Moreover, it would send a cautionary message to Denmark and the other Scandinavian countries not to do any type of business (in the form of non-aggression pacts) with Hitler's Germany.

Scholarship also points to a number of other influences on the subject matter: Grimmelshausen's *Simplicissimus* and *Landstürzen Courage*, picaresque novels about the Thirty Years War published in the late 1660s; Friedrich Schiller's dramatic *Wallenstein* trilogy, published in the 1790s; and Brueghel's painting *Dulle Griet* (1562). From Brecht's own theatrical career, two influences have traditionally been cited: the Widow Begbick character, who turned up in both *Mahagonny* and *A Man's a Man* and was seen as an influence on the Mother Courage character; and Brecht's adaptation of Hasek's *Good Soldier Schweyk* for the Piscator Collective, seen as a source for the artificial dialect used by the characters in *Mother Courage*.

## PERFORMANCE HISTORY

The play premiered at the Zürich Schauspielhaus (Switzerland was a neutral country during the war) in April 1941 under the direction of Leopold Lindtberg, with stage design by Teo Otto and starring Therese Giehse. Brecht was unable to attend due to his wartime exile. The premiere was received well, both critically and popularly, but Brecht was disappointed with the reviews he read that seemed to emphasize the tragic, maternal pathos of Mother Courage as assayed by Therese Giehse. Brecht premiered his own production of *Mother Courage* in Berlin (1949, with Helene Weigel) and Munich (1950, with Giehse again in the main role). The 1949 production used the music of Paul Dessau for the first time and established Weigel as a star actor (if not the one and only Mother Courage), Brecht as a director, and the Berliner Ensemble as a theatre troupe. In the following years, Brecht would develop *Mother Courage* both as a model of Dialectical Theatre practices (organized by Ruth Berlau in *Theaterarbeit*) and as the star production in international tours undertaken by the Berliner Ensemble throughout the 1950s. Weigel's "silent scream" upon hearing of the death of her son Swiss Cheese, and Mother Courage's wagon mounted on a rotating stage became iconic, signature moments associated with the production.

Over the last fifty years, *Mother Courage* has enjoyed notable global premieres and revivals, making it, along with *The Threepenny Opera*, the most canonical Brechtian work. Along with Clytemnestra, Medea, Antigone, Lady Macbeth, and Hedda Gabler, Mother Courage has become one of the great female acting roles on the stage and has been performed by such notable actors as Joan Littlewood, Anne Bancroft, Lotte Lenya, Joan MacIntosh, Olympia Dukakis, Gisela May, Gloria Foster, Linda Hunt, Judi Dench, Eva Mattes, Glenda Jackson, Diana Rigg, Angela Winkler, Carmen-Maja Antoni, and Meryl Streep. In the 2005–06 theatre season alone, as the post–9/11 moment progressed from the War on Terror to the War in Iraq, at least six productions were produced on the world's stages, including the Public Theater's production in New York's Central Park starring Meryl Streep and Kevin Kline, with an adaptation by Tony Kushner.

## THE PROOF OF THE PUDDING: READING *MOTHER COURAGE*

The written *Mother Courage* provides one with a great deal of additional material produced by Brecht between 1939 and 1956, a good part of which is presented in this edition. The reader should consider this material as part of the performance work—a type of dialogue which accompanies the primary text. Since the material is so extensive, one should be judicious if one decides to read it as accompaniment. The following texts are recommended: "The Story: Curve of the Dramaturgy," which is taken from Brecht's *Journals*, and offers pointed aphoristic interventions. The material from "The *Mother Courage* Model" contains a scene-by-scene investigation and is perhaps a bit much to include as performance material. However, if the reader concentrates on the key scenes (1 and 3, 11)—scenes in which her children die—one will be well served by the concise dialectical interplay added to the primary reading.

All adaptations of *Mother Courage*—such as those by Eric Bentley, Marc Blitzstein, Howard Brenton, David Hare, Tony Kushner, and David Edgar, as well as the Willett/Manheim one used in this edition—have noted the difficulty the play presents in its language. It uses neither a historical dialect from the seventeenth century, nor something from Brecht's own dialect reference bank in Germany, ca. 1939; rather, it employs an artificially constructed war jargon. Hence, adapters have chosen different approaches to the translation, using a classical Shakespearean tone, a profane "soldierspeak," or in the case of Willett/Manheim, a "north English cadence" from the adapters' native Great Britain. In general, when reading *Mother Courage* one should consider it an alienated language; in other words, it is a language which is familiar in its clipped, realistic, staccato brutality (which we know from cultural memories of wars and hard life), yet at the same time it is a language which never allows us to get fully comfortable with its rhythms and tones. We never come to rest with Brecht's language—neither the idiomatic, profane language of war, nor the tragic rhetoric of loss, mourning, and suffering.

—NORMAN ROESSLER

# Introduction

That Hitler meant war was clear to Brecht by the beginning of 1937. This was some two and three-quarters years before the Second World War actually broke out. During the previous November the German and Italian fascist regimes had banded together to form the 'Rome-Berlin axis'; Franco, whose rebellious armies were on the outskirts of Madrid, was recognised by them as the legitimate ruler of Spain; an anti-Comintern alliance was forged between Japan, then on the point of invading China, and the Germans. Hitler, who had already got away with the remilitarisation of the Rhineland in defiance of the Versailles Treaty, henceforward had no reason to moderate his aggressive aims. As Brecht put in one of the 'German War Primer' series of poems which he now began writing,

ON THE CALENDAR THE DAY IS NOT YET SHOWN
Every month, every day
Lies open still. One of these days
Is going to be marked with a cross.

For him it was the start of 'The Dark Times': a phrase that from now on permeates his poetry. Living in Denmark on Fünen Island, less than fifty miles across the Baltic from Germany, he could follow the Nazi advance along with the flight from one refuge after another of his own threatened friends: Austria fell in March 1938, the German-speaking areas of Czechoslovakia that September, Prague and the remainder of Czechoslovakia in March 1939, Memel in Lithuania the same month, Madrid and the Spanish Republic with it. Then Hitler offered Denmark a nonaggression pact.

In April 1939, with the Italians in their turn starting to invade Albania, Brecht took advantage of a lecture invitation to move to Sweden, where he was lent a sculptress's house on the island of Lidingö outside Stockholm. From now on he and his immediate entourage were even more isolated than they had been in Denmark; while their object was no longer to await the collapse of the Nazis but to move on to the United States, where Piscator, Fritz Lang and Ferdinand Reyher had already begun working on their behalf. This isolation was also in part political, starting back in 1937 when Brecht largely gave up writing those committed plays and poems which had reflected the day-to-day Communist Party Line. Three things then combined to give him a much more sceptical attitude towards the Soviet Union and Stalin's leadership, which he now thought (as he put it at the beginning of the year) should be like Marx's attitude to the German Socialists of the previous century, 'constructively critical'. The first and most painful of these was the purges of 1936–39, which had led to the death or internment not only of his two main Comintern contacts but also of some of his closest friends. The second, unpleasantly interwoven with the purges, was the imposition of the Socialist Realist aesthetic preached by his old adversary Georg Lukács, which forbade any kind of 'formalism' in the arts; this became a serious factor from 1937 on. Finally there was the switch in foreign policy which led to the Soviet-Nazi pact and the partition of Poland. The Soviet Union, noted Brecht at the time, had thereby saved itself, 'but at the cost of leaving the workers of the world without slogans, hopes or support'.

The day marked with a cross proved to be 1 September 1939, when Brecht somewhat uncharacteristically attended a lunch in honour of Thomas Mann at Stockholm Town Hall. That day the Soviet-Nazi pact was announced, and the Nazis invaded Poland; forty-eight hours later Britain and France declared war. At first Brecht carried on working at his old project *Love Is the Goods*, which he had taken up before leaving Denmark and renamed *The Good Person of Szechwan*; he had also brought with him the unfinished Julius Caesar novel and *The Messingkauf Dialogues*, a by-product of the revision of *Galileo*. But within ten days he found work grinding to a halt. The *Szechwan* play was laid aside; three diary entries comment disillusionedly on the 'singularly Napoleonic' Russian invasion of Eastern Poland, with its 'usurpation of all the Fascist hypocrisy about "blood brotherhood" '; then for nearly seven weeks, from 21 September to 7 November, the diary too goes blank.

During this interval, and in clear reaction to events, Brecht wrote his great play about a war which would range devastatingly across great tracts of Europe, creating heroes and profiteers, imposing order and ideologies, and leaving the self-sentimentalising 'little people'—particularly of Germany—as blindly unaware as they were at its start.

*Mother Courage* was written under pressure. In the words of a later note to Scandinavian audiences,

> As I wrote I imagined that the playwright's warning voice would be heard from the stages of various great cities, proclaiming that he who would sup with the devil must have a long spoon. This may have been naïve of me, but I do not consider being naïve a disgrace. Such productions never materialised. Writers cannot write as rapidly as governments can make war, because writing demands hard thought.

And the effort to speak out quickly made it one of the most spontaneous and, despite its length, most concentrated of all Brecht's plays. It bears virtually no trace of any preliminary work or preparatory reading; there is none of the major rewriting that characterises so many of the other plays: there is for once no mention of any collaborator, nor any element of borrowing or adaptation; there are just two original typescripts, the one a straightforward revise of the other. As a feat of deeply felt anticipation it is amazing. Though there is nothing to bear out Brecht's claim that the play was written in 1938 or (as the note to the 1949 edition had it) 'before the outbreak of the Second World War' it undoubtedly dates from well before the start of any major fighting. This was still the period of 'We'll hang out the washing on the Siegfried Line', of the phoney war, what Brecht termed 'the war that isn't waged'. At that time some kind of peace seemed quite possible, whether as a return to the prewar policy of appeasement or by means of an appeal to the German people over the heads of their government, as wishfully proposed by the Communists. Few foresaw the mass bombings, the deportations, the torture of resistants, the extermination of the Jews; those vast tragedies which any modern audience tends to assume as the understood background to Brecht's 'chronicle play'.

Where did his vision come from? It is rooted, certainly, in his particular feeling for the seventeenth century, the period in which he had already set *The Life of Galileo* with its proclamation of faith in a 'new age' (even if that age might, in the words of the 1938 version, look like 'a bloodstained old harridan'). That last leap forward of the Renaissance—one of whose forms, the Shakespearean History, he adopted for the play—failed in his view to make a modern nation of Germany because of the catastrophic effects of the Thirty Years War, which thus became the natural analogy for his pessimistic warnings. The obvious dramatic precedent here was Schiller's *Wallenstein's Camp* with its picture of a mongrel seventeenth-century army milling round the canteen tents; and indeed there are two engravings showing a camp and Wallenstein's siege of Stralsund in one of the earliest scripts. Stylistically however, and to some extent structurally too, Brecht's example seems to have been the earlier German writer Grimmelshausen, who himself served in the Thirty Years War before publishing his rambling picaresque novel *Simplicissimus* in 1669. From a lesser offshoot of that wartime saga, published separately as *Die Landestörzerin Courasche*, came the name of the play and of its central figure, though in fact Grimmelshausen's Amazonian adventuress sprang from a higher social class than Brecht's canteen woman and enjoyed a career closer to that of Yvette. 'A horrific picture of war,' the critic Bernhard Diebold termed it, 'written about with deliberate detachment and seen from *below*: a frog's-eye view.' The Swedish actress Naima Wifstrand, whom Brecht wanted to play the leading part, also introduced him to the figure of Lotta Svärd, a canteen woman in Johan Ludvig

Runeberg's early-nineteenth-century ballads about the Russian-Swedish war. But she, very unlike Brecht's character, was 'a pearl on the pathway of war', always up with the troops. 'And the dear young soldiers' heroic mood / she loved in its full display.' (Thus G. B. Shaw's translation.)

Brueghel, of whom Brecht had two books of reproductions, may have contributed something; his *Dulle Griet* is gummed into another script—'the Fury', as he described her,

> defending her pathetic household goods with the sword. The world at the end of its tether. Little cruelty, much hypersensitivity.

Callot too is visually relevant, with his *Misères de la Guerre*, even though Brecht nowhere mentions them.

The character of Brecht's Mother Courage, however, like her way of speaking, comes primarily from that other great war novelist Jaroslav Hašek; indeed Brecht saw his own *Schweyk* play, when he came to write it four years later, as a 'companion play'. Moreover there were also other significant links within Brecht's own work. Thus in one sense Mother Courage, battling to save her children, can be compared and contrasted with his earlier Señora Carrar, whom Naima Wifstrand had translated into Swedish and acted. In another she is much closer to the Widow Begbick, the tough itinerant hostess of *Man equals Man* and *Rise and Fall of the City of Mahagonny*, two roles already associated with Helene Weigel. Her language looks forward to the consciously Schweik-like dialogue of *Puntila* and the *Conversations Between Exiles*. And the whole inverted morality of the play, with its suggestion that the conventional virtues sometimes have the opposite effect from what moralists imagine, is close to that of *The Seven Deadly Sins* and *The Threepenny Opera*. This perhaps is why Brecht could think of including 'Surabaya-Johnny' as well as the 'Solomon Song'.

———

Quickly as the play was written, in Brecht's view it came too late to serve as the intended warning. 'The great bandit [i.e., Hitler] got his hooks on the theatres much too soon.' His im-

mediate hope had been that it could be staged in Stockholm
with Wifstrand as Courage and Helene Weigel in the non-
speaking part of Kattrin, who is supposed to have been made
dumb so that Weigel could play her. That winter, while Russia
invaded Finland, Weigel gave some classes in Wifstrand's acting
school, for which Brecht wrote his Shakespearean *Practice
Scenes for Actors*; meanwhile Brecht, on a commission from
Stockholm Radio, wrote *The Trial of Lucullus* for the composer Hilding Rosenberg to set. Given the threat represented
by the Nazis, however, neither work was performed in Sweden;
and in April the police searched the Lidingö house, the German forces moved into Denmark and Norway, and Brecht
thought it wise to move on. The plan for a *Mother Courage*
production was then resumed in Finland, where the Brechts
lived for a further year before the last of the party's American
visas came through. The aim there was to secure a production
in the Helsinki Swedish-language theatre during the winter of
1940–41. To this end. Brecht worked on the songs with the
Finnish composer Simon Parmet, who appears to have dropped
out for fear of echoing Weill too closely. Once again, however,
the reason for the play's rejection was evidently the increasing
Nazi pressure, and that January Brecht listed it as one of his six
unstaged plays 'which cannot at present be performed'.

In German-speaking Switzerland the Zürich Schauspielhaus
was less inhibited. Cut off from the dramatist himself by the
war, this predominantly German company contained a high
proportion of anti-Nazi actors of whom some, like Leonard
Steckel and the director Leopold Lindtberg, had worked in
Berlin with Piscator, while Wolfgang Langhoff had subsequently
been in a concentration camp. Under the sympathetic manage-
ment of Ferdinand Rieser and Oskar Wälterlin they had given the
premières of a number of plays unacceptable in Nazi Germany,
notably Ferdinand Bruckner's *Die Rassen* and Friedrich Wolf's
*Professor Mamlock* (both about anti-Semitism) as well as others
by Kaiser, Horváth, Zuckmayer and such Anglo-American au-
thors as Wilder, O'Neill, Priestley and Shaw. On 19 April 1941,
a month before the Brechts left Helsinki on their long trip to
California, they now gave the première of *Mother Courage* be-

fore a predominantly Swiss and German émigré audience, among those who saw the production being Thornton Wilder.

This was one of the great theatrical events of the Second World War, and the play itself made a great impact, thanks above all to the performance of Therese Giehse (who oddly enough was a British subject) in the title part and to the setting devised by Teo Otto, who had worked with Brecht before 1933. Lindtberg directed, and the Swiss composer Paul Burkhard wrote a new score. Langhoff and the Austrian Karl Paryla played the two sons, Wolfgang Heinz the cook. Meanwhile Sigfrit Steiner, the Chaplain of this production, was staging the far more directly political *Mother* for the first time in Switzerland with a cast of amateurs. And yet Brecht, appreciative as he was, felt that to some extent his intentions had been traduced. Thus Bernhard Diebold, who had been one of the outstanding German theatre critics before 1933, wrote in *Die Tat* that this *Courage*, far from being a 'hyaena of the battlefield' (as the Chaplain calls her), made her commercial toughness 'almost too subsidiary' to the strength of her maternal feelings; while as for Lindtberg's direction, it 'either failed to take enough account of the crude earthiness of the period and Brecht's own malicious sarcasm, or else it deliberately softened them'.

As it turned out, this was the play's sole wartime production. It was not one of these works which Brecht expected to see put on in the USA, nor did he make any of the efforts which he and his friends there devoted to *Fear and Misery of the Third Reich*, *Galileo* and *The Good Person of Szechwan*, let alone the plays which he wrote after arriving. Early in 1941, at the latest, the poet H. R. Hays had made a translation from a copy lent him by Hanns Eisler (to whom Brecht sent one of the first scripts), but although this appeared in *New Directions* the same year there never seems to have been any move to stage it, not even as a college production. Almost it might be said that Brecht had decided to shelve *Mother Courage* as he shelved so many of his works, putting them out of his mind for years at a time. In 1943, however, he met the composer Paul Dessau, whose musical background was in some ways comparable to those of Weill and Eisler, and who had written some music for the original

Paris production of *Fear and Misery of the Third Reich* in which Weigel had acted. At a Brecht recital given at the New School in New York that March, Dessau sang one of his own Brecht settings with such verve that Brecht encouraged him to write more, first inviting him to come and work in California, then at some undefined date asking him to write new settings for the *Mother Courage* songs. These were completed by 1946, when the Zürich company used them for its guest performances in Vienna, and they became the standard music for the play. For the moment it seems that they, like the play itself, were really being reserved for the day when Brecht should return to the German-language theatre and stage the kind of performance which he and Helene Weigel had in mind.

Though there is evidence in the FBI files of his intention to return from as early as 1944, it seems to have been at least a year after the ending of the war that he began to make serious plans. Then he wrote to his old collaborator the designer Caspar Neher (who had remained in Germany) to announce his conviction that 'we shall build up a theatre once more', followed by his decision to come to Zürich during 1947 and prepare his return to Berlin, where he had been offered the use of the Theater am Schiffbauerdamm 'for certain things'. This theatre, the original home of *The Threepenny Opera*, had now been made an offshoot of the revived Volksbühne, the great popular theatre organisation which the Nazis had suppressed thirteen years earlier. The Deutsches Theater, where Brecht had worked for Max Reinhardt on first coming to Berlin, had been put under Langhoff of the Zürich *Mother Courage*; both theatres were in the Soviet sector.

Early in 1947 Brecht and Piscator started corresponding with a view to a joint descent on that city. They were in some measure encouraged in this by Friedrich Wolf, who had returned with the Red Army and now hoped to draw Piscator back to the Volksbühne. Before Piscator made up his mind, however, the division of Berlin had occurred, and in the event he remained in New York for another three years. Meanwhile the Brechts carried out their plan of going to Zürich, and immediately on arrival began discussing plans with Neher. Within a month the two friends in collaboration had completed the adaptation of *Antigone* which they proposed to stage at the small theatre in Chur managed by Klemperer's former dramaturg Hans Curjel. The object of this brilliant but short-lived exercise, so Brecht noted in his diary on 16 December, was 'to do preparatory work with Weigel and Cas [Neher] on *Courage* for Berlin'. For Weigel had not acted on the professional stage for fifteen years, and the Schauspielhaus apparently had nothing for her.

The *Antigone* production took place on 15 February 1948, five days after Brecht's fiftieth birthday. The same occasion was celebrated in Berlin by a programme organised by Langhoff, who had staged a short version of *Fear and Misery of the Third Reich* only a fortnight or so earlier. Thereafter it was agreed that the Zürich Schauspielhaus would give the first production of *Puntila*, the fourth and last of their Brecht premières and the first to be staged with Brecht's own participation (as unofficial director); this took place in June, with Leonard Steckel acting the name part. After that the Brechts' attention was again focused on Berlin (Salzburg being an alternative bet), and the main problem was how to get there. Eventually the necessary Austrian and Czech permits came through, allowing them to travel to the Soviet Zone of Germany in late October (the U.S. authorities having refused them leave to cross Bavaria). Straightaway Brecht began holding auditions at Langhoff's theatre, then on 8 November his co-director Erich Engel arrived from Munich and two months of intensive rehearsal began. Brecht's idea at this time was to set up his own ensemble under the wing of the Deutsches Theater and invite prominent outsiders to act with it; he had in mind figures like Fritz Kortner and Peter Lorre as well as Therese Giehse from Zürich.

In mid-December he discussed this scheme with Langhoff, seemingly still in the expectation of being able to use the Theater am Schiffbauerdamm. Then three weeks later he was hauled out of a rehearsal to attend a formal meeting with the party authorities, the East Berlin mayor Friedrich Ebert (son of the former Social-Democratic President), Langhoff and the Schiffbauerdamm *Intendant* Fritz Wisten. Here he was told that the Schiffbauerdamm was needed for the Volksbühne; the mayor, who never addressed a word to him, spoke slightingly of half-baked schemes which might upset existing arrangements; and, in the words of the diary, 'for the first time since coming here I felt the foetid breath of provincialism'.

Within a few days, however, everything fell into the background as the white half-curtain of the Deutsches Theater fluttered open on a brilliantly lit stage. The band struck up 'You captains, tell the drums to slacken', and the dusty, tattered family came rolling on with its cart. Suddenly, in this still devastated city hovering between peace and war, the world could see one of the unforgettable images of our time.

———

From that moment dates Brecht's postwar reputation as a great director, which for non-Germans has even overshadowed his reputation as a playwright. It was a formidable comeback planned from three overlapping aspects, and its triple success was stunning. First of all, here was a largely unknown German masterpiece, written in language of tremendous vitality and still with many shrewd things to say about war and people's reactions to it. Second was an outstanding acting performance from a virtually forgotten actress, whose striking voice and features have become almost inseparable from the Mother Courage figure; that night a legendary character, as well as a star, was born. Finally, embracing everything else, there was a new, outwardly subdued but inwardly authoritative spirit emanating from the whole company and from the new Berliner Ensemble which the Brechts went on to found upon it. The object of this entire operation was of course rather different from Brecht's original aim when he wrote the play. For he made it very clear in his notes and jottings that he wished not only to make his countrymen think about their blind involvement in Hitler's war but also to help rebuild their shattered culture and bridge the long gap back to the progressive ideas of the Weimar Republic, thereby bringing on a new generation of actors and directors who would not have been debased by too much experience of Nazi methods. Given that he meant to tackle these worthwhile tasks from within the Communist orbit, in his old spirit of sceptical allegiance, he had to establish his constructive intentions, which he set himself to do soon after his arrival by writing some slightly vapid political songs. At the same time he had to overcome or get round the obstacles to any kind of formal innovation embodied in the revived Socialist Realism now being preached by the Russians and, once again, Georg Lukács. As he put it in the foreword to *Antigone*, 'it may not be easy to create progressive art in the period of reconstruction'. But nobody was now better placed to do it than he.

The criticisms of the play which now came from both right and left arose from a feeling that Brecht, having created a great human character, had deliberately stunted her, thereby stifling much of the emotion natural both to himself as the creator and also to his audience. Some, like Friedrich Wolf in the dialogue printed on pp. 226–9 of *Brecht on Theatre*, felt that by the end of the play Courage should have seen the light—that is, the futility of war—thereby emerging as (in Communist aesthetic jargon) a 'positive' figure. Others, on both sides of the barriers, pointed to what they considered a theoretical inconsistency between Brecht's ideas of 'epic' or 'alienated' acting and the undoubted empathy experienced by audiences at emotional high spots like the death of Kattrin. This notion that Brecht, for purely intellectual reasons, was denying certain powerful elements which he had (or should have) instinctively put into the original play, was reinforced, if not actually sparked off, by the textual changes which he confesses to on pp. 89–92 of his notes. Indeed to judge from some commentators' reactions one might imagine that he had rewritten the Zürich version as extensively as he did so many of his other plays. In fact, of course, only two of his four alterations are significant—the first, where Courage's salesmanship distracts her from her son's enlistment, and the second, which makes her less ready than before to give her goods for humanitarian ends—and they would scarcely have been noticed if he had not drawn attention to them himself. What he worked much harder to correct was not any 'softness' in the actual play but those features of Lindtberg's production on which Diebold had commented nearly eight years earlier, along with a certain 'curious aura of harmlessness' which he found emanating from his own first Berlin rehearsals. This, with its smudging-over of all sense of background or development, he blamed on the bland conformism of the Nazi theatre.

But it is true that the point of the play had in some measure changed, and the audiences who saw it in Berlin and Munich (where he re-staged it with Giehse as Courage and a new cast), or during the Berliner Ensemble's various tours, were very different from that in wartime Zürich. For these people had been through a European war; they did not have to be warned about it; they were actually beginning to experience the consequences, including some which Brecht had not foretold. Nonetheless he remained convinced that his countrymen were a long way from understanding how far they had contributed to the horror, the chaos and the suffering—their own included. Doubtful whether they had learnt anything, he was convinced that it would be misleading to make Courage finish up any less short-sighted than they. In fact the surprising thing, to anyone familiar with Brecht's restless revaluation of his own plays, is that he did not alter the text more. Perhaps the reason for this is that his chronic itch to revise could in this case be worked out on the (alas, unrealised) film version, whose making by the East German DEFA was decided as early as September 1949. Initially the work on its script was done by Emil Hesse Burri, Brecht's old collaborator of the mid-1920s, who had been a scriptwriter in Munich under the Nazis; and the intention was that Engel should direct it. When Engel fell out some time during 1951 he was replaced by the forty-five-year-old Wolfgang Staudte, a former Piscator trainee whose DEFA film *Die Mörder sind unter uns* had been the first great postwar success. Though Brecht himself did not actually do any of the writing, he was in on the planning, and many of the changes were in line with his suggestions. The film, said his first notes for DEFA, 'must bring out even more clearly than the play how reality punishes [Mother Courage] for her failure to learn'. The treatment was simplified to distinguish her from the 'little people' and show her marked urge to go forward and profit from the war; later the 'little people' too were criticised as 'the worst of the lot. Why? The big shots plan it, and the little people carry it out'. Kattrin in turn was given a lover, a young miller whose vision of popular resistance to the rulers and their foreign mercenaries is echoed during the scene of her death, when the peasants in the besieged town take up improvised arms and drive out the attackers (now made Croats in order to seem more alien). This is clearly in accordance with the criticisms made of the play by Wolf and others, who wanted a greater element of optimism at the end; though the old woman herself, her eyes lighting up 'with an expression of greed and desperate hope' as she hears the troops marching off, finishes up more incorrigible than ever. After Burri had completed this first script he and Brecht agreed to make the story more relevant to the postwar occupation of Germany by stressing the contrast between the German protagonists (Eilif and Yvette were now to be Germans, like Courage and Kattrin) and their motley foreign invaders; there would be control barriers everywhere and a 'Babylonian' mixture of strange tongues. Evidence too would be given of persistent foreign attempts to recruit Germans (including the young miller) for continued wars. Brecht's feelings at this point are well summed up in the poem 'Germany 1952' which was worked into the final script, where a group of deserters led by the young miller throw down their weapons in an abandoned house full of bourgeois comforts and one of them sings:

> O Germany, so torn in pieces
> And never left alone!
> The cold and dark increases
> While each sees to his own.
> Such lovely fields you'd have
> Such cities thronged and gay;
> If you'd but trust yourself
> All would be child's play.

But this film was never made. The trouble seems to have been that DEFA, instead of setting out from the Brecht-Engel production and the actors associated with it, wished to make a grand international co-production with star appeal. Simone Signoret was booked as Yvette, whose part was then disproportionately inflated; the French actor Bernard Blier became the cook. Angelika Hurwicz, the unforgettable stage Kattrin, was replaced by Sigrid Roth; difficulties were made over Helene Weigel, who had to be cast as Courage on Brecht's insistence. In many other ways, too, Brecht's vision and Staudte's proved deeply incompatible. Staudte wanted to use colour, Brecht to achieve 'daguerreotype-like effects in black and white; Staudte commissioned period costumes, Brecht rejected them as too operatic; Staudte's French designer provided the heavy baronial setting seen in the surviving stills and located the camp scenes in a sandy waste, Brecht objected that the Thirty Years War didn't take place in a desert. Staudte's verdict was that Brecht was 'utterly hostile to the cinema'. Shooting nevertheless began, apparently on the assumption that Brecht would feel forced to accept designs which had only been put before him at the very last moment. He did not, and as a result the whole operation had to be called off after about a fortnight's unhappy work. It was never resumed, though plans for some kind of *Mother Courage* film continued to be discussed, this time with Engel and Burri, right up to Brecht's death in August 1956. The film which DEFA did finally realise some four years later was made on an entirely different basis, for it was a largely static film version, made in a studio and photographed in Cinemascope, of the Berliner Ensemble stage production: a kind of Model-book in motion, preserving Brecht's original vision with minor changes. Its directors were Brecht's young assistants Manfred Wekwerth and Peter Palitzsch, who subsequently directed, respectively, the Berliner Ensemble itself and the Frankfurt city theatres.

———

It was one of Brecht's endless inconsistencies (or 'contradictions') that, while believing firmly in the need for change, he established certain standard productions which other directors of his plays were expected to study before deciding their own interpretations. *Mother Courage* was a prime candidate for this treatment, thanks on the one hand to its high reputation with other theatres throughout the globe and on the other to the critical disagreements which it provoked. The 'Mother Courage Model' therefore consists not only of the notes which we print on pp. 91–135 but of a series of carefully-keyed photographs of the Berliner Ensemble production which exists in a published version but was originally made as a much fuller and more detailed album for loan to prospective directors. Brecht's purpose here has often been regarded as absurdly rigid, and the Ensemble itself has been accused of putting Brecht's works into some kind of airless museum showcase. On the one hand there have been instances of lifeless copying or resentful friction whenever the standard model was imposed; on the other it has shocked more jealously 'original' producers to go as far as they can in some alternative, if not actually opposite, direction. Seldom has any director done what Brecht really had in mind: that is, gone through the 'model' to see exactly what problems Brecht was trying to solve in each detail of his production, and how he arrived at his answers, and then gone on to think out an approach of his own based on the same understanding of the play. So the use of Model-books has proved to be a somewhat two-edged device, hindering as much as helping the assimilation of this great play, particularly by non-German theatres.

Certainly *Mother Courage* has never become securely established in the English-speaking countries, where the size of the cast and the length of the play present a more formidable initial problem than they do in the German subsidised theatres. Generally it has proved a box-office disaster, and the one production to enjoy a long run—Richard Schechner's with the Performance Group off-Broadway—seems to have done so more because of its original treatment of the audience than by its conception and performance of the text; it became a vivid, sharply biting Courage experience, almost a happening. The odd thing is that this overall failure in the professional theatre has not impaired the play's critical and academic reputation, nor even its attraction for amateurs, to whom of course a large cast often seems an advantage. As a result *Mother Courage* is still somehow lurking in the wings as an enormous challenge, even something of a reproach to our finest directors and actors. Why have they never been able to communicate its pessimism, its savagery and its force? A large part of the reason surely lies in the language, which in the original is unique, the invention of a major poet who chose neither to imitate seventeenth-century dialogue nor to reproduce modern everyday speech but devised his own curt, sardonic lingo, full of elisions and with few conjunctions, vividly conveying not only Courage's own character but also the hard pressures of the war. This is established in the very first speeches, and from then on it becomes the principal dynamic force of what is otherwise a stragglingly episodic play. Those directors who have enough German to appreciate it have generally treated it as untranslatable, thereby losing their main chance of holding the audience's attention; the sense has been communicated at the cost of Brecht's imaginative assault on the ear. Our translation therefore sets out to tackle this key problem by using a somewhat analogous artificial diction, based this time on those north English cadences which can reflect a similarly dry, gloomily humorous approach to great events. It could have been done in other ways—by a Welsh or Irish writer perhaps, or one versed in Lallans—but so far it has not. The aim must be to find a language which will keep the play moving across twelve years of history, a great slice of devastated Europe and, last but not least, three or four hours in the theatre.

Add this to the barriers sometimes presented by the 'Model', plus the widespread feeling among actors that performing Brecht demands outlandish technical methods, and there is some danger of *Mother Courage* appearing a horribly complicated play. You only have to read it to see that it is not. Even the changes which Brecht made to it are only designed to clarify and bring out more strongly what was already meant to be there; they were correctives, not major switches of direction. All this belongs in the background, to be digested and understood certainly, but not to obstruct the story of the play and the long chain of small, conflicting episodes which goes to make it up. The stage must be cleared, as Brecht cleared it in 1950 to tell German children 'The story of Mother Courage':

There once was a mother
Mother Courage they called her
In the Thirty Years War
She sold victuals to soldiers.

The war did not scare her
From making her cut
Her three children went with her
And so got their bit.

Her first son died a hero
The second an honest lad
A bullet found her daughter
Whose heart was too good.

In the end it has to be as simple as that.

**THE EDITORS**

# Characters

MOTHER COURAGE
KATTRIN, *her dumb daughter*
EILIF, *the elder son*
SWISS CHEESE, *the younger son*
THE RECRUITER
THE SERGEANT
THE COOK
THE GENERAL
THE CHAPLAIN
THE ARMOURER
YVETTE POTTIER
THE MAN WITH THE PATCH
ANOTHER SERGEANT
THE ANCIENT COLONEL
A CLERK
A YOUNG SOLDIER
AN OLDER SOLDIER
A PEASANT
THE PEASANT'S WIFE
THE YOUNG MAN
THE OLD WOMAN
ANOTHER PEASANT
HIS WIFE
THE YOUNG PEASANT
THE ENSIGN
SOLDIERS
A VOICE

# Mother Courage and
# Her Children

# I

SPRING 1624. THE SWEDISH COMMANDER-IN-CHIEF
COUNT OXENSTIERNA IS RAISING TROOPS IN
DALECARLIA FOR THE POLISH CAMPAIGN. THE
CANTEEN WOMAN ANNA FIERLING, KNOWN UNDER
THE NAME OF MOTHER COURAGE, LOSES ONE SON.

*Country road near a town.*
*A sergeant and a recruiter stand shivering.*

RECRUITER: How can you muster a unit in a place like this?
I've been thinking about suicide, sergeant. Here am I, got to
find our commander four companies before the twelfth of the
month, and people round here are so nasty I can't sleep
nights. S'pose I get hold of some bloke and shut my eye to his
pigeon chest and varicose veins, I get him proper drunk, he
signs on the line, I'm just settling up, he goes for a piss, I follow him to the door because I smell a rat; bob's your uncle,
he's off like a flea with the itch. No notion of word of honour, loyalty, faith, sense of duty. This place has shattered my
confidence in the human race, sergeant.

SERGEANT: It's too long since they had a war here; stands to
reason. Where's their sense of morality to come from? Peace
—that's just a mess; takes a war to make order. Peacetime, the human race runs wild. People and cattle get bug-
gered about, who cares? Everyone eats just as he feels
inclined, a hunk of cheese on top of his nice white bread, and
a slice of fat on top of the cheese. How many young blokes
and good horses in that town there, nobody knows; they
never thought of counting. I been in places ain't seen a war
for nigh seventy years: folks hadn't got names to them,
couldn't tell one another apart. Takes a war to get proper
nominal rolls and inventories—shoes in bundles and corn in

bags, and man and beast properly numbered and carted off, cause it stands to reason: no order, no war.

RECRUITER: Too true.

SERGEANT: Same with all good things, it's a job to get a war going. But once it's blossomed out there's no holding it; folk start fighting shy of peace like punters what can't stop for fear of having to tot up what they lost. Before that it's war they're fighting shy of. It's something new to them.

RECRUITER: Hey, here's a cart coming. Two tarts with two young fellows. Stop her, sergeant. If this one's a flop I'm not standing around in your spring winds any longer, I can tell you.

*Sound of a jew's-harp. Drawn by two young fellows, a covered cart rolls in. On it sit Mother Courage and her dumb daughter Kattrin.*

MOTHER COURAGE: Morning, sergeant.

SERGEANT *blocking the way*: Morning, all. And who are you?

MOTHER COURAGE: Business folk. *Sings:*

> You captains, tell the drums to slacken
> And give your infanteers a break:
> It's Mother Courage with her waggon
> Full of the finest boots they make.
> With crawling lice and looted cattle
> With lumbering guns and straggling kit—
> How can you flog them into battle
> Unless you get them boots that fit?
>> The new year's come. The watchmen shout.
>> The thaw sets in. The dead remain.
>> Wherever life has not died out
>> It staggers to its feet again.
>
> Captains, how can you make them face it—
> Marching to death without a brew?
> Courage has rum with which to lace it
> And boil their souls and bodies through.
> Their musket primed, their stomach hollow—
> Captains, your men don't look so well.

So feed them up and let them follow
While you command them into hell.
 The new year's come. The watchmen shout.
 The thaw sets in. The dead remain.
 Wherever life has not died out
 It staggers to its feet again.

SERGEANT: Halt! Who are you with, you trash?

THE ELDER SON: Second Finnish Regiment.

SERGEANT: Where's your papers?

MOTHER COURAGE: Papers?

THE YOUNGER SON: What, mean to say you don't know Mother Courage?

SERGEANT: Never heard of her. What's she called Courage for?

MOTHER COURAGE: Courage is the name they gave me because I was scared of going broke, sergeant, so I drove me cart right through the bombardment of Riga with fifty loaves of bread aboard. They were going mouldy, it was high time, hadn't any choice really.

SERGEANT: Don't be funny with me. Your papers.

MOTHER COURAGE *pulling a bundle of papers from a tin box and climbing down off the cart*: That's all my papers, sergeant. You'll find a whole big missal from Altötting in Bavaria for wrapping gherkins in, and a road map of Moravia, the Lord knows when I'll ever get there, might as well chuck it away, and here's a stamped certificate that my horse hasn't got foot-and-mouth, only he's dead worse luck, cost fifteen florins he did—not me luckily. That enough paper for you?

SERGEANT: You pulling my leg? I'll knock that sauce out of you. S'pose you know you got to have a licence.

MOTHER COURAGE: Talk proper to me, do you mind, and don't you dare say I'm pulling your leg in front of my unsullied children, 'tain't decent, I got no time for you. My honest face, that's me licence with the Second Regiment, and if it's too difficult for you to read there's nowt I can do about it. Nobody's putting a stamp on that.

RECRUITER: Sergeant, methinks I smell insubordination in this individual. What's needed in our camp is obedience.

MOTHER COURAGE: Sausage, if you ask me.

SERGEANT: Name.

MOTHER COURAGE: Anna Fierling.

SERGEANT: You all called Fierling then?

MOTHER COURAGE: What d'you mean? It's me's called Fierling, not them.

SERGEANT: Aren't all this lot your children?

MOTHER COURAGE: You bet they are, but why should they all have to be called the same, eh? *Pointing to her elder son:* For instance, that one's called Eilif Nojocki—Why? his father always claimed he was called Kojocki or Mojocki or something. The boy remembers him clearly, except that the one he remembers was someone else, a Frenchie with a little beard. Aside from that he's got his father's wits; that man knew how to snitch a peasant's pants off his bum without him noticing. This way each of us has his own name, see.

SERGEANT: What, each one different?

MOTHER COURAGE: Don't tell me you ain't never come across that.

SERGEANT: So I s'pose he's a Chinaman? *Pointing to the younger son.*

MOTHER COURAGE: Wrong. Swiss.

SERGEANT: After the Frenchman?

MOTHER COURAGE: What Frenchman? I never heard tell of no Frenchman. You keep muddling things up, we'll be hanging around here till dark. A Swiss, but called Fejos, and the name has nowt to do with his father. He was called something quite different and was a fortifications engineer, only drunk all the time.

*Swiss Cheese beams and nods; dumb Kattrin too is amused.*

SERGEANT: How in hell can he be called Fejos?

MOTHER COURAGE: I don't like to be rude, sergeant, but you ain't got much imagination, have you? Course he's called Fejos, because when he arrived I was with a Hungarian, very decent fellow, had terrible kidney trouble though he never touched a drop. The boy takes after him.

SERGEANT: But he wasn't his father . . .

MOTHER COURAGE: Took after him just the same. I call him

Swiss Cheese. *Pointing to her daughter:* And that's Kattrin Haupt, she's half German.

SERGEANT: Nice family, I must say.

MOTHER COURAGE: Aye, me cart and me have seen the world.

SERGEANT: I'm writing all this down. *He writes.* And you're from Bamberg in Bavaria; how d'you come to be here?

MOTHER COURAGE: Can't wait till war chooses to visit Bamberg, can I?

RECRUITER *to Eilif:* You two should be called Jacob Ox and Esau Ox, pulling the cart like that. I s'pose you never get out of harness?

EILIF: Ma, can I clobber him one? I wouldn't half like to.

MOTHER COURAGE: And I says you can't; just you stop where you are. And now two fine officers like you, I bet you could use a good pistol, or a belt buckle, yours is on its last legs, sergeant.

SERGEANT: I could use something else. Those boys are healthy as young birch trees, I observe: chests like barrels, solid leg muscles. So why are they dodging their military service, may I ask?

MOTHER COURAGE *quickly:* Nowt doing, sergeant. Yours is no trade for my kids.

RECRUITER: But why not? There's good money in it, glory too. Flogging boots is women's work. *To Eilif:* Come here, let's see if you've muscles in you or if you're a chicken.

MOTHER COURAGE: He's a chicken. Give him a fierce look, he'll fall over.

RECRUITER: Killing a young bull that happens to be in his way. *Wants to lead him off.*

MOTHER COURAGE: Let him alone, will you? He's nowt for you folk.

RECRUITER: He was crudely offensive and talked about clobbering me. The two of us are going to step into that field and settle it man to man.

EILIF: Don't you worry, mum, I'll fix him.

MOTHER COURAGE: Stop there! You varmint! I know you, nowt but fights. There's a knife down his boot. A slasher, that's what he is.

RECRUITER: I'll draw it out of him like a milk-tooth. Come along, sonny.

MOTHER COURAGE: Sergeant, I'll tell the colonel. He'll have you both in irons. The lieutenant's going out with my daughter.

SERGEANT: No rough stuff, chum. *To Mother Courage:* What you got against military service? Wasn't his own father a soldier? Died a soldier's death, too? Said it yourself.

MOTHER COURAGE: He's nowt but a child. You want to take him off to slaughterhouse, I know you lot. They'll give you five florins for him.

RECRUITER: First he's going to get a smart cap and boots, eh?

EILIF: Not from you.

MOTHER COURAGE: Let's both go fishing, said angler to worm. *To Swiss Cheese:* Run off, call out they're trying to kidnap your brother. *She pulls a knife:* Go on, you kidnap him, just try. I'll slit you open, trash. I'll teach you to make war with him. We're doing an honest trade in ham and linen, and we're peaceable folk.

SERGEANT: Peaceable I don't think; look at your knife. You should be ashamed of yourself; put that knife away, you old harridan. A minute back you were admitting you live off the war, how else should you live, what from? But how's anyone to have war without soldiers?

MOTHER COURAGE: No need for it to be my kids.

SERGEANT: Oh, you'd like war to eat the pips but spit out the apple? It's to fatten up your kids, but you won't invest in it. Got to look after itself, eh? And you called Courage, fancy that. Scared of the war that keeps you going? Your sons aren't scared of it, I can see that.

EILIF: Take more than a war to scare me.

SERGEANT: And why? Look at me: has army life done all that badly by me? Joined up at seventeen.

MOTHER COURAGE: Still got to reach seventy.

SERGEANT: I don't mind waiting.

MOTHER COURAGE: Under the sod, eh?

SERGEANT: You trying to insult me, saying I'll die?

MOTHER COURAGE: S'pose it's true? S'pose I can see the mark's on you? S'pose you look like a corpse on leave to me? Eh?

SWISS CHEESE: She's got second sight, Mother has.

RECRUITER: Go ahead, tell the sergeant's fortune, might amuse him.

MOTHER COURAGE: Gimme helmet. *He gives it to her.*

SERGEANT: It don't mean a bloody sausage. Anything for a laugh though.

MOTHER COURAGE *taking out a sheet of parchment and tearing it up*: Eilif, Swiss Cheese and Kattrin, may all of us be torn apart like this if we lets ourselves get too mixed up in the war. *To the Sergeant:* Just for you I'm doing it for free. Black's for death. I'm putting a big black cross on this slip of paper.

SWISS CHEESE: Leaving the other one blank, see?

MOTHER COURAGE: Then I fold them across and shake them. All of us is jumbled together like this from our mother's womb, and now draw a slip and you'll know. *The Sergeant hesitates.*

RECRUITER *to Eilif*: I don't take just anybody, they all know I'm choosey, but you got the kind of fire I like to see.

SERGEANT *fishing in the helmet*: Too silly. Load of eyewash.

SWISS CHEESE: Drawn a black cross, he has. Write him off.

RECRUITER: They're having you on; not everybody's name's on a bullet.

SERGEANT *hoarsely*: You've put me in the shit.

MOTHER COURAGE: Did that yourself the day you became a soldier. Come along, let's move on now. 'Tain't every day we have a war, I got to get stirring.

SERGEANT: God damn it, you can't kid me. We're taking that bastard of yours for a soldier.

EILIF: Swiss Cheese'd like to be a soldier too.

MOTHER COURAGE: First I've heard of that. You'll have to draw too, all three of you. *She goes to the rear to mark crosses on further slips.*

RECRUITER *to Eilif*: One of the things they say against us is that it's all holy-holy in the Swedish camp; but that's a malicious rumour to do us down. There's no hymn-singing but Sundays, just a single verse, and then only for those got voices.

MOTHER COURAGE *coming back with the slips, which she drops into the sergeant's helmet*: Trying to get away from their ma, the devils, off to war like calves to salt-lick. But I'm making you draw lots, and that'll show you the world is no vale of joys with 'Come along, son, we need a few more generals'. Sergeant, I'm so scared they won't get through the war. Such dreadful characters, all three of them. *She hands the helmet to Eilif.* Hey, come on, fish out your slip. *He fishes one out, unfolds it. She snatches it from him.* There you are, it's a cross. Oh, wretched mother that I am, oh pain-racked giver of birth! Shall he die? Aye, in the springtime of life he is doomed. If he becomes a soldier he shall bite the dust, it's plain to see. He is too foolhardy, like his dad was. And if he ain't sensible he'll go the way of all flesh, his slip proves it. *Shouts at him:* You going to be sensible?

EILIF: Why not?

MOTHER COURAGE: Sensible thing is stay with your mother, never mind if they poke fun at you and call you chicken, just you laugh.

RECRUITER: If you're pissing in your pants I'll make do with your brother.

MOTHER COURAGE: I told you laugh. Go on, laugh. Now you draw, Swiss Cheese. I'm not so scared on your account, you're honest. *He fishes in the helmet.* Oh, why look at your slip in that strange way? It's got to be a blank. There can't be any cross on it. Surely I'm not going to lose *you.* *She takes the slip.* A cross? What, you too? Is that because you're so simple, perhaps? Oh Swiss Cheese, you too will be sunk if you don't stay utterly honest all the while, like I taught you from childhood when you brought the change back from the baker's. Else you can't save yourself. Look, sergeant, that's a black cross, ain't it?

SERGEANT: A cross, that's right. Can't think how I come to get one. I always stay in the rear. *To the recruiter:* There's no catch. Her own family get it too.

SWISS CHEESE: I get it too. But I listen to what I'm told.

MOTHER COURAGE *to Kattrin*: And now you're the only one I know's all right, you're a cross yourself; got a kind heart you have. *Holds the helmet up to her on the cart, but takes the slip out herself.* No, that's too much. That can't be right; must have made a mistake shuffling. Don't be too kind-hearted, Kattrin, you'll have to give it up, there's a cross above your path too. Lie doggo, girl, it can't be that hard once you're born dumb. Right, all of you know now. Look out for yourselves, you'll need to. And now up we get and on we go. *She climbs on to the cart.*

RECRUITER *to the sergeant*: Do something.

SERGEANT: I don't feel very well.

RECRUITER: Must of caught a chill taking your helmet off in that wind. Involve her in a deal. *Aloud:* Might as well have a look at that belt-buckle, sergeant. After all, our friends here have to live by their business. Hey, you people, the sergeant wants to buy that belt-buckle.

MOTHER COURAGE: Half a florin. Two florins is what a belt like that's worth. *Climbs down again.*

SERGEANT: 'Tain't new. Let me get out of this damned wind and have a proper look at it. *Goes behind the cart with the buckle.*

MOTHER COURAGE: Ain't what I call windy.

SERGEANT: I s'pose it might be worth half a florin, it's silver.

MOTHER COURAGE *joining him behind the cart*: It's six solid ounces.

RECRUITER *to Eilif*: And then we men'll have one together. Got your bounty money here, come along. *Eilif stands undecided.*

MOTHER COURAGE: Half a florin it is.

SERGEANT: It beats me. I'm always at the rear. Sergeant's the safest job there is. You can send the others up front, cover themselves with glory. Me dinner hour's properly spoiled. Shan't be able to hold nowt down, I know.

MOTHER COURAGE: Mustn't let it prey on you so's you can't eat. Just stay at the rear. Here, take a swig of brandy, man. *Gives him a drink.*

RECRUITER *has taken Eilif by the arm and is leading him away up stage*: Ten florins bounty money, then you're a gallant fellow fighting for the king and women'll be after you like flies. And you can clobber me for free for insulting you. *Exeunt both.*

*Dumb Kattrin leans down from the cart and makes hoarse noises.*

MOTHER COURAGE: All right, Kattrin, all right. Sergeant's just paying. *Bites the half-florin.* I got no faith in any kind of money. Burnt child, that's me, sergeant. This coin's good, though. And now let's get moving. Where's Eilif?

SWISS CHEESE: Went off with the recruiter.

MOTHER COURAGE *stands quite still, then*: You simpleton. *To Kattrin:* 'Tain't your fault, you can't speak, I know.

SERGEANT: Could do with a swig yourself, ma. That's life. Plenty worse things than being a soldier. Want to live off war, but keep yourself and family out of it, eh?

MOTHER COURAGE: You'll have to help your brother pull now, Kattrin.

*Brother and sister hitch themselves to the cart and start pulling. Mother Courage walks alongside. The cart rolls on.*

SERGEANT *looking after them*:

Like the war to nourish you?
Have to feed it something too.

# 2

IN THE YEARS 1625 AND 1626 MOTHER COURAGE
CROSSES POLAND IN THE TRAIN OF THE SWEDISH
ARMIES. BEFORE THE FORTRESS OF WALLHOF SHE
MEETS HER SON AGAIN. SUCCESSFUL SALE OF A
CAPON AND HEYDAY OF HER DASHING SON.

*The general's tent.*

*Beside it, his kitchen. Thunder of cannon. The cook is arguing
with Mother Courage, who wants to sell him a capon.*

THE COOK: Sixty hellers for a miserable bird like that?

MOTHER COURAGE: Miserable bird? This fat brute? Mean to
say some greedy old general—and watch your step if you got
nowt for his dinner—can't afford sixty hellers for him?

THE COOK: I can get a dozen like that for ten hellers just down
the road.

MOTHER COURAGE: What, a capon like this you can get just
down the road? In time of siege, which means hunger that tears
your guts. A rat you might get: 'might' I say because they're all
being gobbled up, five men spending best part of day chasing
one hungry rat. Fifty hellers for a giant capon in time of siege!

THE COOK: But it ain't us having the siege, it's t'other side.
We're conducting the siege, can't you get that in your head?

MOTHER COURAGE: But we got nowt to eat too, even worse
than them in the town. Took it with them, didn't they?
They're having a high old time, everyone says. And look at
us! I been to the peasants, there's nowt there.

THE COOK: There's plenty. They're sitting on it.

MOTHER COURAGE *triumphantly*: They ain't. They're bust,
that's what they are. Just about starving. I saw some, were
grubbing up roots from sheer hunger, licking their fingers

after they boiled some old leather strap. That's way it is. And
me got a capon here and supposed to take forty hellers for it.

THE COOK: Thirty, not forty. I said thirty.

MOTHER COURAGE: Here, this ain't just any old capon. It was
such a gifted beast, I been told, it could only eat to music,
had a military march of its own. It could count, it was that
intelligent. And you say forty hellers is too much? General
will make mincemeat of you if there's nowt on his table.

THE COOK: See what I'm doing? *He takes a piece of beef and
puts his knife to it.* Here I got a bit of beef, I'm going to roast
it. Make up your mind quick.

MOTHER COURAGE: Go on, roast it. It's last year's.

THE COOK: Last night's. That animal was still alive and kicking, I saw him myself.

MOTHER COURAGE: Alive and stinking, you mean.

THE COOK: I'll cook him five hours if need be. I'll just see if
he's still tough. *He cuts into it.*

MOTHER COURAGE: Put plenty of pepper on it so his lordship
the general don't smell the pong.

*The general, a chaplain and Eilif enter the tent.*

THE GENERAL *slapping Eilif on the shoulder*: Now then, Eilif
my son, into your general's tent with you and sit thou at my
right hand. For you accomplished a deed of heroism, like a pi-
ous cavalier, and doing what you did for God, and in a war of
religion at that, is something I commend in you most highly,
you shall have a gold bracelet as soon as we've taken this town.
Here we are, come to save their souls for them, and what do
those insolent dung-encrusted yokels go and do? Drive their
beef away from us. They stuff it into those priests of theirs all
right, back and front, but you taught 'em manners, ha! So
here's a pot of red wine for you, the two of us'll knock it back
at one gulp. *They do so.* Piss all for the chaplain, the old bigot.
And now, what would you like for dinner, my darling?

EILIF: A bit of meat, why not?

THE GENERAL: Cook! Meat!

THE COOK: And then he goes and brings guests when there's
nowt there.

*Mother Courage silences him so she can listen.*

EILIF: Hungry job cutting down peasants.

MOTHER COURAGE: Jesus Christ, it's my Eilif.

THE COOK: Your what?

MOTHER COURAGE: My eldest boy. It's two years since I lost
sight of him, they pinched him from me on the road, must
think well of him if the general's asking him to dinner, and
what kind of a dinner can you offer? Nowt. You heard what
the visitor wishes to eat: meat. Take my tip, you settle for the
capon, it'll be a florin.

THE GENERAL *has sat down with Eilif, and bellows*: Food,
lamb, you foul cook, or I'll have your hide.

THE COOK: Give it over, dammit, this is blackmail.

MOTHER COURAGE: Didn't someone say it was a miserable
bird?

THE COOK: Miserable; give it over, and a criminal price, fifty
hellers.

MOTHER COURAGE: A florin, I said. For my eldest boy, the
general's guest, no expense is too great for me.

THE COOK *gives her the money*: You might at least pluck it
while I see to the fire.

MOTHER COURAGE *sits down to pluck the fowl*: He won't half
be surprised to see me. He's my dashing clever son. Then I
got a stupid one too, he's honest though. The girl's nowt.
One good thing, she don't talk.

THE GENERAL: Drink up, my son, this is my best Falernian;
only got a barrel or two left, but that's nothing to pay for a
sign that there's still true faith to be found in my army. As for
that shepherd of souls he can just look on, because all he does
is preach, without the least idea how it's to be carried out.
And now, my son Eilif, tell us more about the neat way you
smashed those yokels and captured the twenty oxen. Let's
hope they get here soon.

EILIF: A day or two at most.

MOTHER COURAGE: Thoughtful of our Eilif not to bring the
oxen in till tomorrow, else you lot wouldn't have looked
twice at my capon.

EILIF: Well, it was like this, see. I'd heard peasants had been driving the oxen they'd hidden, out of the forest into one particular

wood, on the sly and mostly by night. That's where people from the town were s'posed to come and pick them up. So I holds off and lets them drive their oxen together, reckoning they'd be better than me at finding 'em. I had my blokes slavering after the meat, cut their emergency rations even further for a couple of days till their mouths was watering at the least sound of any word beginning with 'me-', like 'measles' say.

THE GENERAL: Very clever of you.

EILIF: Possibly. The rest was a piece of cake. Except that the peasants had cudgels and outnumbered us three to one and made a murderous attack on us. Four of 'em shoved me into a thicket, knocked my sword from my hand and bawled out 'Surrender!' What's the answer, I wondered; they're going to make mincemeat of me.

THE GENERAL: What did you do?

EILIF: I laughed.

THE GENERAL: You did what?

EILIF: Laughed. So we got talking. I put it on a business footing from the start, told them 'Twenty florins a head's too much. I'll give you fifteen'. As I was meaning to pay. That threw them, and they began scratching their heads. In a flash I'd picked up my sword and was hacking 'em to pieces. Necessity's the mother of invention, eh, sir?

THE GENERAL: What is your view, pastor of souls?

THE CHAPLAIN: That phrase is not strictly speaking in the Bible, but when Our Lord turned the five loaves into five hundred there was no war on and he could tell people to love their neighbours as they'd had enough to eat. Today it's another story.

THE GENERAL *laughs*: Quite another story. You can have a swig after all for that, you old Pharisee. *To Eilif:* Hacked 'em to pieces, did you, so my gallant lads can get a proper bite to eat? What do the Scriptures say? 'Whatsoever thou doest for the least of my brethren, thou doest for me'. And what did you do for them? Got them a good square meal of beef, because they're not accustomed to mouldy bread, the old way was to fix a cold meal of rolls and wine in your helmet before you went out to fight for God.

EILIF: Aye, in a flash I'd picked up my sword and was hacking them to pieces.

THE GENERAL: You've the makings of a young Caesar. You ought to see the King.

EILIF: I have from a distance. He kind of glows. I'd like to model myself on him.

THE GENERAL: You've got something in common already. I appreciate soldiers like you, Eilif, men of courage. Somebody like that I treat as I would my own son. *He leads him over to the map.* Have a look at the situation, Eilif; it's a long haul still.

MOTHER COURAGE *who has been listening and now angrily plucks the fowl*: That must be a rotten general.

THE COOK: He's ravenous all right, but why rotten?

MOTHER COURAGE: Because he's got to have men of courage, that's why. If he knew how to plan a proper campaign what would he be needing men of courage for? Ordinary ones would do. It's always the same; whenever there's a load of special virtues around it means something stinks.

THE COOK: I thought it meant things is all right.

MOTHER COURAGE: No, that they stink. Look, s'pose some general or king is bone stupid and leads his men up shit creek, then those men've got to be fearless, there's another virtue for you. S'pose he's stingy and hires too few soldiers, they they got to be a crowd of Herculeses. And s'pose he's slapdash and don't give a bugger, then they got to be clever as monkeys else their number's up. Same way they got to show exceptional loyalty each time he gives them impossible jobs. Nowt but virtues no proper country and no decent king or general would ever need. In decent countries folk don't have to have virtues, the whole lot can be perfectly ordinary, average intelligence, and for all I know cowards.

THE GENERAL: I'll wager your father was a soldier.

EILIF: A great soldier, I been told. My mother warned me about it. There's a song I know.

THE GENERAL: Sing it to us. *Roars:* When's that dinner coming?
EILIF: It's called The Song of the Girl and the Soldier.
   *He sings it, dancing a war dance with his sabre:*

   The guns blaze away, and the bay'nit'll slay
   And the water can't hardly be colder.
   What's the answer to ice? Keep off's my advice!
   That's what the girl told the soldier.
   Next thing the soldier, wiv' a round up the spout
   Hears the band playing and gives a great shout:
   Why, it's marching what makes you a soldier!
   So it's down to the south and then northwards once more:
   See him catching that bay'nit in his naked paw!
   That's what his comrades done told her.

   Oh, do not despise the advice of the wise
   Learn wisdom from those that are older
   And don't try for things that are out of your reach—
   That's what the girl told the soldier.
   Next thing the soldier, his bay'nit in place
   Wades into the river and laughs in her face
   Though the water comes up to his shoulder.
   When the shingle roof glints in the light o' the moon
   We'll be wiv' you again, not a moment too soon!
   That's what his comrades done told her.

MOTHER COURAGE *takes up the song in the kitchen, beating
   on a pot with her spoon:*

   You'll go out like a light! And the sun'll take flight
   For your courage just makes us feel colder.
   Oh, that vanishing light! May God see that it's right!—
   That's what the girl told the soldier.

EILIF: What's that?

MOTHER COURAGE *continues singing:*

Next thing the soldier, his bay'nit in place
Was caught by the current and went down without trace
And the water couldn't hardly be colder.
The shingle roof froze in the light o' the moon
As both soldier and ice drifted down to their doom—
And d'you know what his comrades done told her?

He went out like a light. And the sunshine took flight
For his courage just made 'em feel colder.
Oh, do not despise the advice of the wise!
That's what the girl told the soldier.

THE GENERAL: The things they get up to in my kitchen these
days.

EILIF *has gone into the kitchen. He flings his arms round his
mother*: Fancy seeing you again, ma! Where's the others?

MOTHER COURAGE *in his arms*: Snug as a bug in a rug. They
made Swiss Cheese paymaster of the Second Finnish; any
road he'll stay out of fighting that way, I couldn't keep him
out altogether.

EILIF: How's the old feet?

MOTHER COURAGE: Bit tricky getting me shoes on of a morning.

THE GENERAL *has joined them*: So you're his mother, I hope
you've got plenty more sons for me like this one.

EILIF: Ain't it my lucky day? You sitting out there in the
kitchen, ma, hearing your son commended . . .

MOTHER COURAGE: You bet I heard. *Slaps his face.*

EILIF *holding his cheek*: What's that for? Taking the oxen?

MOTHER COURAGE: No. Not surrendering when those four
went for you and wanted to make mincemeat of you. Didn't I
say you should look after yourself? You Finnish devil!

*The general and the chaplain stand in the doorway laughing.*

# 3

*Military camp.*
*Afternoon. A flagpole with the regimental flag. From her cart,
festooned now with all kinds of goods, Mother Courage has
stretched a washing line to a large cannon, across which she
and Kattrin are folding the washing. She is bargaining at the
same time with an armourer over a sack of shot. Swiss Cheese,
now wearing a paymaster's uniform, is looking on.*

*A comely person, Yvette Pottier, is sewing a gaily coloured
hat, a glass of brandy before her. She is in her stockinged feet,
having laid aside her red high-heeled boots.*

THE ARMOURER: I'll let you have that shot for a couple of
florins. It's cheap at the price, I got to have the money because the colonel's been boozing with his officers since two
days back, and the drink's run out.

MOTHER COURAGE: That's troops' munitions. They catch me
with that, I'm for court-martial. You crooks flog the shot, and
troops got nowt to fire at enemy.

THE ARMOURER: Have a heart, can't you; you scratch my back
and I'll scratch yours.

MOTHER COURAGE: I'm not taking army property. Not at that
price.

THE ARMOURER: You can sell it on the q.t. tonight to the
Fourth Regiment's armourer for five florins, eight even, if
you let him have a receipt for twelve. He's right out of ammunition.

MOTHER COURAGE: Why not you do it?

THE ARMOURER: I don't trust him, he's a pal of mine.

MOTHER COURAGE *takes the sack*: Gimme. *To Kattrin*: Take it away and pay him a florin and a half. *The armourer protests.* I said a florin and a half. *Kattrin drags the sack upstage, the armourer following her. Mother Courage addresses Swiss Cheese*: Here's your woollies, now look after them, it's October and autumn may set in any time. I ain't saying it's got to, 'cause I've learned nowt's got to come when you think it will, not even seasons of the year. But your regimental accounts got to add up right, come what may. Do they add up right?

SWISS CHEESE: Yes, mother.

MOTHER COURAGE: Don't you forget they made you paymaster cause you was honest, not dashing like your brother, and above all so stupid. I bet you ain't even thought of clearing off with it, no not you. That's a big consolation to me. And don't lose those woollies.

SWISS CHEESE: No, mother, I'll put them under my mattress. *Begins to go.*

THE ARMOURER: I'll go along with you, paymaster.

MOTHER COURAGE: And don't you start learning him none of your tricks.

*The armourer leaves with Swiss Cheese without any farewell gesture.*

YVETTE *waving to him*: No reason not to say goodbye, armourer.

MOTHER COURAGE *to Yvette*: I don't like to see them together. He's wrong company for our Swiss Cheese. Oh well, war's off to a good start. Easily take four, five years before all countries are in. A bit of foresight, don't do nothing silly, and business'll flourish. Don't you know you ain't s'posed to drink before midday with your complaint?

YVETTE: Complaint, who says so, it's a libel.

MOTHER COURAGE: They all say so.

YVETTE: Because they're all telling lies, Mother Courage, and me at my wits' end cause they're all avoiding me like something the cat brought in thanks to those lies, what the hell am

I remodelling my hat for? *She throws it away.* That's why I drink before midday. Never used to, gives you crows' feet, but now what the hell? All the Second Finnish know me. Ought to have stayed at home when my first fellow did me wrong. No good our sort being proud. Eat shit, that's what you got to do, or down you go.

MOTHER COURAGE: Now don't you start up again about that Pieter of yours and how it all happened, in front of my innocent daughter too.

YVETTE: She's the one should hear it, put her off love.

MOTHER COURAGE: Nobody can put 'em off that.

YVETTE: Then I'll go on, get it off my chest. It all starts with yours truly growing up in lovely Flanders, else I'd never of seen him and wouldn't be stuck here now in Poland, cause he was an army cook, fair-haired, a Dutchman but thin for once. Kattrin, watch out for the thin ones, only in those days I didn't know that, or that he'd got a girl already, or that they all called him Puffing Piet cause he never took his pipe out of his mouth when he was on the job, it meant that little to him. *She sings the Song of Fraternisation:*

> When I was only sixteen
> The foe came into our land.
> He laid aside his sabre
> And with a smile he took my hand.
> After the May parade
> The May light starts to fade.
> The regiment dressed by the right
> The drums were beaten, that's the drill.
> The foe took us behind the hill
> And fraternised all night.
>
> There were so many foes then
> But mine worked in the mess.
> I loathed him in the daytime.
> At night I loved him none the less.
> After the May parade
> The May light starts to fade.

The regiment dressed by the right
The drums were beaten, that's the drill.
The foe took us behind the hill
And fraternised all night.

The love which came upon me
Was wished on me by fate.
My friends could never grasp why
I found it hard to share their hate.
The fields were wet with dew
When sorrow first I knew.
The regiment dressed by the right
The drums were beaten, that's the drill.
And then the foe, my lover still
Went marching out of sight.

I followed him, fool that I was, but I never found him, and
that was five years back. *She walks unsteadily behind the cart.*

MOTHER COURAGE: You left your hat here.

YVETTE: Anyone wants it can have it.

MOTHER COURAGE:  Let that be a lesson, Kattrin. Don't you
start anything with them soldiers. Love makes the world go
round, I'm warning you. Even with fellows not in the army it's
no bed of roses. He says he'd like to kiss the ground your feet
walk on—reminds me, did you wash them yesterday?—and after that you're his skivvy. Be thankful you're dumb, then you
can't contradict yourself and won't be wanting to bite your
tongue off for speaking the truth; it's a godsend, being dumb
is. And here comes the general's cook, now what's he after?
*Enter the cook and the chaplain.*

THE CHAPLAIN: I have a message for you from your son Eilif,
and the cook has come along because you made such a profound impression on him.

THE COOK: I just came along to get a bit of air.

MOTHER COURAGE: That you can always do here if you behave
yourself, and if you don't I can deal with you. What does he
want? I got no spare cash.

THE CHAPLAIN: Actually I had a message for his brother the paymaster.

MOTHER COURAGE: He ain't here now nor anywhere else neither. He ain't his brother's paymaster. He's not to lead him into temptation nor be clever at his expense. *Giving him money from the purse slung round her:* Give him this, it's a sin, he's banking on mother's love and ought to be ashamed of himself.

THE COOK: Not for long, he'll have to be moving off with the regiment, might be to his death. Give him a bit extra, you'll be sorry later. You women are tough, then later on you're sorry. A little glass of brandy wouldn't have been a problem, but it wasn't offered and, who knows, a bloke may lie beneath the green sod and none of you people will ever be able to dig him up again.

THE CHAPLAIN: Don't give way to your feelings, cook. To fall in battle is a blessing, not an inconvenience, and why? It is a war of faith. None of your common wars but a special one, fought for the faith and therefore pleasing to God.

THE COOK: Very true. It's a war all right in one sense, what with requisitioning, murder and looting and the odd bit of rape thrown in, but different from all the other wars because it's a war of faith; stands to reason. But it's thirsty work at that, you must admit.

THE CHAPLAIN *to Mother Courage, indicating the cook*: I tried to stop him, but he says he's taken a shine to you, you figure in his dreams.

THE COOK *lighting a stumpy pipe*: Just want a glass of brandy from a fair hand, what harm in that? Only I'm groggy already cause the chaplain here's been telling such jokes all the way along you bet I'm still blushing.

MOTHER COURAGE: Him a clergyman too. I'd best give the pair of you a drink or you'll start making me immoral suggestions cause you've nowt else to do.

THE CHAPLAIN: Behold a temptation, said the court preacher, and fell. *Turning back to look at Kattrin as he leaves:* And who is this entrancing young person?

MOTHER COURAGE: That ain't an entrancing but a decent

young person. *The chaplain and the cook go behind the cart with Mother Courage. Kattrin looks after them, then walks away from her washing towards the hat. She picks it up and sits down, pulling the red boots towards her. Mother Courage can be heard in the background talking politics with the chaplain and the cook.*

MOTHER COURAGE: Those Poles here in Poland had no business sticking their noses in. Right, our king moved in on them, horse and foot, but did they keep the peace? No, went and stuck their noses into their own affairs, they did, and fell on the king just as he was quietly clearing off. They committed a breach of peace, that's what, so blood's on their own head.

THE CHAPLAIN: All our king minded about was freedom. The emperor had made slaves of them all, Poles and Germans alike, and the king had to liberate them.

THE COOK: Just what I say, your brandy's first rate, I weren't mistaken in your face, but talk of the king, it cost the king dear trying to give freedom to Germany, what with giving Sweden the salt tax, what cost the poor folk a bit, so I've heard, on top of which he had to have the Germans locked up and drawn and quartered 'cause they wanted to carry on slaving for the emperor. Course the king took a serious view when anybody didn't want to be free. He set out by just trying to project Poland against bad people, particularly the emperor, then it started to become a habit till he ended up protecting the whole of Germany. They didn't half kick. So the poor old king's had nowt but trouble for all his kindness and expenses, and that's something he had to make up for by taxes of course, which caused bad blood, not that he's let a little matter like that depress him. One thing he had on his side, God's word, that was a help. Because otherwise folk would of been saying he done it all for himself and to make a bit on the side. So he's always had a good conscience, which was the main point.

MOTHER COURAGE: Anyone can see you're no Swede or you wouldn't be talking that way about the Hero King.

THE CHAPLAIN: After all he provides the bread you eat.

THE COOK: I don't eat it, I bake it.

MOTHER COURAGE: They'll never beat him, and why, his men got faith in him. *Seriously:* To go by what the big shots say, they're waging war for almighty God and in the name of everything that's good and lovely. But look closer, they ain't so silly, they're waging it for what they can get. Else little folk like me wouldn't be in it at all.

THE COOK: That's the way it is.

THE CHAPLAIN: As a Dutchman you'd do better to glance at the flag above your head before venting your opinions here in Poland.

MOTHER COURAGE: All good Lutherans here. Prosit!
*Kattrin has put on Yvette's hat and begun strutting around in imitation of her way of walking.*

*Suddenly there is a noise of cannon fire and shooting. Drums. Mother Courage, the cook and the chaplain rush out from behind the cart, the two last-named still carrying their glasses. The armourer and another soldier run up to the cannon and try to push it away.*

MOTHER COURAGE: What's happening? Wait till I've taken my washing down, you louts! *She tries to rescue her washing.*

THE ARMOURER: The Catholics! Broken through. Don't know if we'll get out of here. *To the soldier:* Get that gun shifted! *Runs on.*

THE COOK: God, I must find the general. Courage, I'll drop by in a day or two for another talk.

MOTHER COURAGE: Wait, you forgot your pipe.

THE COOK *in the distance*: Keep it for me. I'll be needing it.

MOTHER COURAGE: Would happen just as we're making a bit of money.

THE CHAPLAIN: Ah well, I'll be going too. Indeed, if the enemy is so close as that it might be dangerous. Blesséd are the peacemakers is the motto in wartime. If only I had a cloak to cover me.

MOTHER COURAGE: I ain't lending no cloaks, not on your life. I been had too often.

THE CHAPLAIN: But my faith makes it particularly dangerous for me.

MOTHER COURAGE *gets him a cloak*: Goes against my conscience, this does. Now you run along.

THE CHAPLAIN: Thank you, dear lady, that's very generous of
you, but I think it might be wiser for me to remain seated
here; it could arouse suspicion and bring the enemy down on
me if I were seen to run.

MOTHER COURAGE *to the soldier*: Leave it, you fool, who's going to pay you for that? I'll look after it for you, you're risking your neck.

THE SOLDIER *running away*: You can tell 'em I tried.

MOTHER COURAGE: Cross my heart. *Sees her daughter with
the hat*. What you doing with that strumpet's hat? Take that
lid off, you gone crazy? And the enemy arriving any minute!
*Pulls the hat off Kattrin's head*. Want 'em to pick you up and
make a prostitute of you? And she's gone and put those boots
on, whore of Babylon! Off with those boots! *Tries to tug
them off her*. Jesus Christ, chaplain, gimme a hand, get those
boots off her, I'll be right back. *Runs to the cart*.

YVETTE *arrives, powdering her face*: Fancy that, the Catholics
are coming. Where's my hat? Who's been kicking it around?
I can't go about looking like this if the Catholics are coming.
What'll they think of me? No mirror either. *To the chaplain*:
How do I look? Too much powder?

THE CHAPLAIN: Exactly right.

YVETTE: And where are them red boots? *Fails to find them as
Kattrin hides her feet under her skirt*. I left them here all
right. Now I'll have to get to me tent barefoot. It's an outrage. *Exit*.

*Swiss Cheese runs in carrying in a small box*.

MOTHER COURAGE *arrives with her hands full of ashes*. *To
Kattrin*: Here are some ashes. *To Swiss Cheese*: What's that
you're carrying?

SWISS CHEESE: Regimental cash box.

MOTHER COURAGE: Chuck it away. No more paymastering
for you.

SWISS CHEESE: I'm responsible. *He goes to the rear*.

MOTHER COURAGE *to the chaplain*: Take your clerical togs
off, padre, or they'll spot you under that cloak. *She rubs Kat-*

*trin's face with ash.* Keep still, will you? There you are, a bit of muck and you'll be safe. What a disaster. Sentries were drunk. Hide your light under a bushel, it says. Take a soldier, specially a Catholic one, add a clean face, and there's your instant whore. For weeks they get nowt to eat, then soon as they manage to get it by looting they're falling on anything in skirts. That ought to do. Let's have a look. Not bad. Looks like you been grubbing in a muckheap. Stop trembling. Nothing'll happen to you like that. *To Swiss Cheese:* Where d'you leave the cash box?

SWISS CHEESE: Thought I'd put it in cart.

MOTHER COURAGE *horrified*: What, my cart? Sheer criminal idiocy. Only take me eyes off you one instant. Hang us all three, they will.

SWISS CHEESE: I'll put it somewhere else then, or clear out with it.

MOTHER COURAGE: You sit on it, it's too late now.

CHAPLAIN *who is changing his clothes downstairs*: For heaven's sake, the flag!

MOTHER COURAGE *hauls down the regimental flag*: Bozhe moi! I'd given up noticing it were there. Twenty-five years I've had it.

*The thunder of cannon intensifies.*

*A morning three days later. The cannon has gone. Mother Courage, Kattrin, the chaplain and Swiss Cheese are sitting gloomily over a meal.*

SWISS CHEESE: That's three days I been sitting around with nowt to do, and sergeant's always been kind to me but any moment now he'll start asking where's Swiss Cheese with the pay box?

MOTHER COURAGE: You thank your stars they ain't after you.

THE CHAPLAIN: What can I say? I can't even hold a service here, it might make trouble for me. Whosoever hath a full heart, his tongue runneth over, it says, but heaven help me if mine starts running over.

MOTHER COURAGE: That's how it goes. Here they sit, one
with his faith and the other with his cash box. Dunno which
is more dangerous.

THE CHAPLAIN: We are all of us in God's hands.

MOTHER COURAGE: Oh, I don't think it's as bad as that yet,
though I must say I can't sleep nights. If it weren't for you,
Swiss Cheese, things'd be easier. I think I got meself cleared.
I told 'em I didn't hold with Antichrist, the Swedish one with
horns on, and I'd observed the left horn was a bit unser-
viceable. Half way through their interrogation I asked where
I could get church candles not too dear. I knows the lingo
'cause Swiss Cheese's dad were Catholic, often used to make
jokes about it, he did. They didn't believe me all that much,
but they ain't got no regimental canteen lady. So they're
winking an eye. Could turn out for the best, you know. We're
prisoners, but same like fleas on dog.

THE CHAPLAIN: That's good milk. But we'll need to cut down
our Swedish appetites a bit. After all, we've been defeated.

MOTHER COURAGE: Who's been defeated? Look, victory and
defeat ain't bound to be same for the big shots up top as for
them below, not by no means. Can be times the bottom lot
find a defeat really pays them. Honour's lost, nowt else. I remember once up in Livonia our general took such a beating
from the enemy I got a horse off our baggage train in the
confusion, pulled me cart seven months, he did, before we
won and they checked up. As a rule you can say victory and
defeat both come expensive to us ordinary folk. Best thing
for us is when politics get bogged down solid. *To Swiss
Cheese:* Eat up.

SWISS CHEESE: Got no appetite for it. What's sergeant to do
when pay day comes round?

MOTHER COURAGE: They don't have pay days on a retreat.

SWISS CHEESE: It's their right, though. They needn't retreat if
they don't get paid. Needn't stir a foot.

MOTHER COURAGE: Swiss Cheese, you're that conscientious it
makes me quite nervous. I brought you up to be honest, you
not being clever, but you got to know where to stop. Chaplain

and me, we're off now to buy Catholic flag and some meat. Dunno anyone so good at sniffing meat, like sleepwalking it is, straight to target. I'd say he can pick out a good piece by the way his mouth starts watering. Well, thank goodness they're letting me go on trading. You don't ask tradespeople their faith but their prices. And Lutheran trousers keep cold out too.

THE CHAPLAIN: What did the mendicant say when he heard the Lutherans were going to turn everything in town and country topsy-turvy? They'll always need beggars. *Mother Courage disappears into the cart.* So she's still worried about the cash box. So far they've taken us all for granted as part of the cart, but how long for?

SWISS CHEESE: I can get rid of it.

THE CHAPLAIN: That's almost more dangerous. Suppose you're seen. They have spies. Yesterday a fellow popped up out of the ditch in front of me just as I was relieving myself first thing. I was so scared I only just suppressed an ejaculatory prayer. That would have given me away all right. I think what they'd like best is to go sniffing people's excrement to see if they're Protestants. The spy was a little runt with a patch over one eye.

MOTHER COURAGE *clambering out of the cart with a basket*: What have I found, you shameless creature? *She holds up the red boots in triumph.* Yvette's red high-heeled boots! Coolly went and pinched them, she did. 'Cause you put it in her head she was an enchanting young person. *She lays them in the basket.* I'm giving them back. Stealing Yvette's boots! She's wrecking herself for money. That's understandable. But you'd do it for nothing, for pleasure. What did I tell you: you're to wait till it's peace. No soldiers for you. You're not to start exhibiting yourself till it's peacetime.

THE CHAPLAIN: I don't find she exhibits herself.

MOTHER COURAGE: Too much for my liking. Let her be like a stone in Dalecarlia, where there's nowt else, so folk say 'Can't see that cripple', that's how I'd lief have her. Then nowt'll happen to her. *To Swiss Cheese:* You leave that box where it is, d'you hear? And keep an eye on your sister, she

needs it. The pair of you'll have me in grave yet. Sooner be
minding a bagful of fleas.

*She leaves with the chaplain. Kattrin clears away the dishes.*

SWISS CHEESE: Won't be able to sit out in the sun in shirt-
sleeves much longer. *Kattrin points at a tree.* Aye, leaves
turning yellow. *Kattrin asks by gestures if he wants a drink.*
Don't want no drink. I'm thinking. *Pause.* Said she can't
sleep. Best if I got rid of that box, found a good place for it.
All right, let's have a glass. *Kattrin goes behind the cart.* I'll
stuff it down the rat-hole by the river for the time being.
Probably pick it up tonight before first light and take it to
Regiment. How far can they have retreated in three days? Bet
sergeant's surprised. I'm agreeably disappointed in you,
Swiss Cheese, he'll say. I make you responsible for the cash,
and you go and bring it back.

*As Kattrin emerges from behind the cart with a full glass in
her hand, two men confront her. One is a sergeant, the other
doffs his hat to her. He has a patch over one eye.*

THE MAN WITH THE PATCH: God be with you, mistress. Have
you seen anyone round here from Second Finnish Regimental
Headquarters?

*Kattrin, badly frightened, runs downstage, spilling the
brandy. The two men look at one another, then withdraw on
seeing Swiss Cheese sitting there.*

SWISS CHEESE *interrupted in his thoughts*: You spilt half of it.
What are those faces for? Jabbed yourself in the eye? I don't
get it. And I'll have to be off, I've thought it over, it's the
only way. *He gets up. She does everything possible to make
him realise the danger. He only shrugs her off.* Wish I knew
what you're trying to say. Sure you mean well, poor creature, just can't get words out. What's it matter your spilling
my brandy, I'll drink plenty more glasses yet, what's one
more or less? *He gets the box from the cart and takes it under his tunic.* Be back in a moment. Don't hold me up now,
or I'll be angry. I know you mean well. Too bad you can't
speak.

*As she tries to hold him back he kisses her and tears himself
away. Exit. She is desperate, running hither and thither*

*uttering little noises. The chaplain and Mother Courage return. Kattrin rushes to her mother.*

MOTHER COURAGE: What's all this? Pull yourself together, love. They done something to you? Where's Swiss Cheese? Tell it me step by step, Kattrin. Mother understands you. What, so that bastard did take the box? I'll wrap it round his ears, the little hypocrite. Take your time and don't gabble, use your hands, I don't like it when you howl like a dog, what'll his reverence say? Makes him uncomfortable. What, a one-eyed man came along?

THE CHAPLAIN: That one-eyed man is a spy. Have they arrested Swiss Cheese? *Kattrin shakes her head, shrugs her shoulders.* We're done for.

MOTHER COURAGE *fishes in her basket and brings out a Catholic flag, which the chaplain fixes to the mast*: Better hoist new flag.

THE CHAPLAIN *bitterly*: All good Catholics here.

*Voices are heard from the rear. The two men bring in Swiss Cheese.*

SWISS CHEESE: Let me go, I got nowt. Don't twist my shoulder, I'm innocent.

SERGEANT: Here's where he came from. You know each other.

MOTHER COURAGE: Us? How?

SWISS CHEESE: I don't know her. Got no idea who she is, had nowt to do with them. I bought me dinner here, ten hellers it cost. You might have seen me sitting here, it was too salty.

SERGEANT: Who are you people, eh?

MOTHER COURAGE: We're law-abiding folk. That's right, he bought a dinner. Said it was too salty.

SERGEANT: Trying to pretend you don't know each other, that it?

MOTHER COURAGE: Why should I know him? Can't know everyone. I don't go asking 'em what they're called and are they a heretic; if he pays he ain't a heretic. You a heretic?

SWISS CHEESE: Go on.

THE CHAPLAIN: He sat there very properly, never opening his mouth except when eating. Then he had to.

SERGEANT: And who are you?

MOTHER COURAGE: He's just my potboy. Now I expect you gentlemen are thirsty, I'll get you a glass of brandy, you must be hot and tired with running.

SERGEANT: No brandy on duty. *To Swiss Cheese:* You were carrying something. Must have hidden it by the river. Was a bulge in your tunic when you left here.

MOTHER COURAGE: You sure it was him?

SWISS CHEESE: You must be thinking of someone else. I saw someone bounding off with a bulge in his tunic. I'm the wrong man.

MOTHER COURAGE: I'd say it was a misunderstanding too, such things happen. I'm a good judge of people, I'm Courage, you heard of me, everyone knows me, and I tell you that's an honest face he has.

SERGEANT: We're on the track of the Second Finnish Regiment's cash box. We got the description of the fellow responsible for it. Been trailing him two days. It's you.

SWISS CHEESE: It's not me.

SERGEANT: And you better cough it up, or you're a goner, you know. Where is it?

MOTHER COURAGE *urgently*: Of course he'd give it over rather than be a goner. Right out he'd say: I got it, here it is, you're too strong. He ain't all that stupid. Speak up, stupid idiot, here's the sergeant giving you a chance.

SWISS CHEESE: S'pose I ain't got it.

SERGEANT: Then come along. We'll get it out of you. *They lead him off.*

MOTHER COURAGE *calls after them*: He'd tell you. He's not that stupid. And don't you twist his shoulder! *Runs after them.*

*Evening of the same day. The chaplain and dumb Kattrin are cleaning glasses and polishing knives.*

THE CHAPLAIN: Cases like that, where somebody gets caught, are not unknown in religious history. It reminds me of the Passion of Our Lord and Saviour. There's an old song about that. *He sings the Song of the Hours:*

In the first hour Jesus mild
Who had prayed since even
Was betrayed and led before
Pontius the heathen.

Pilate found him innocent
Free from fault and error
Therefore, having washed his hands
Sent him to King Herod.

In the third hour he was scourged
Stripped and clad in scarlet
And a plaited crown of thorns
Set upon his forehead.

On the Son of Man they spat
Mocked him and made merry.
Then the cross of death was brought
Given him to carry.

At the sixth hour with two thieves
To the cross they nailed him
And the people and the thieves
Mocked him and reviled him.

This is Jesus King of Jews
Cried they in derision
Till the sun withdrew its light
From that awful vision.

At the ninth hour Jesus wailed
Why hast thou me forsaken?
Soldiers brought him vinegar
Which he left untaken.

Then he yielded up the ghost
And the earth was shaken.
Rended was the temple's veil
And the saints were wakened.

Soldiers broke the two thieves' legs
As the night descended
Thrust a spear in Jesus' side
When his life had ended.

Still they mocked, as from his wound
Flowed the blood and water
Thus blasphemed the Son of Man
With their cruel laughter.*

MOTHER COURAGE *entering excitedly*: It's touch and go. They say sergeant's open to reason though. Only we mustn't let on it's Swiss Cheese else they'll say we helped him. It's a matter of money, that's all. But where's money to come from? Hasn't Yvette been round? I ran into her, she's got her hooks on some colonel, maybe he'd buy her a canteen business.

THE CHAPLAIN: Do you really wish to sell?

MOTHER COURAGE: Where's money for sergeant to come from?

THE CHAPLAIN: What'll you live on, then?

MOTHER COURAGE: That's just it.

*Yvette Pottier arrives with an extremely ancient colonel.*

YVETTE *embracing Mother Courage*: My dear Courage, fancy seeing you so soon. *Whispers:* He's not unwilling. *Aloud:* This is my good friend who advises me in business matters. I happened to hear you wanted to sell your cart on account of circumstances. I'll think it over.

MOTHER COURAGE: Pledge it, not sell, just not too much hurry, tain't every day you find a cart like this in wartime.

YVETTE *disappointed*: Oh, pledge. I though it was for sale. I'm not so sure I'm interested. *To the colonel:* How do you feel about it?

THE COLONEL: Just as you feel, pet.

MOTHER COURAGE: I'm only pledging it.

YVETTE: I thought you'd got to have the money.

*Song translated by Ralph Manheim.

MOTHER COURAGE *firmly*: I got to have it, but sooner run my-self ragged looking for a bidder than sell outright. And why? The cart's our livelihood. It's a chance for you, Yvette; who knows when you'll get another like it and have a special friend to advise you, am I right?

YVETTE: Yes, my friend thinks I should clinch it, but I'm not sure. If it's only a pledge . . . so you agree we ought to buy outright?

THE COLONEL: I agree, pet.

MOTHER COURAGE: Best look and see if you can find anything for sale then; maybe you will if you don't rush it, take your friend along with you, say a week or fortnight, might find something suits you.

YVETTE: Then let's go looking. I adore going around looking for things, I adore going around with you, Poldi, it's such fun, isn't it? No matter if it takes a fortnight. How soon would you pay the money back if you got it?

MOTHER COURAGE: I'd pay back in two weeks, maybe one.

YVETTE: I can't make up my mind, Poldi chéri, you advise me. *Takes the colonel aside:* She's got to sell, I know, no prob-lem there. And there's that ensign, you know, the fair-haired one, he'd be glad to lend me the money. He's crazy about me, says there's someone I remind him of. What do you advise?

THE COLONEL: You steer clear of him. He's no good. He's only making use of you. I said I'd buy you something, didn't I, pussykins?

YVETTE: I oughtn't to let you. Of course if you think the ensign might try to take advantage . . . Poldi, I'll accept it from you.

THE COLONEL: That's how I feel too.

YVETTE: Is that your advice?

THE COLONEL: That is my advice.

YVETTE *to Courage once more*: My friend's advice would be to accept. Make me out a receipt saying the cart's mine once two weeks are up, with all its contents, we'll check it now, I'll bring the two hundred florins later. *To the colonel:* You go back to the camp, I'll follow, I got to check it all and see there's nothing missing from my cart. *She kisses him. He*

*leaves. She climbs up on the cart.* Not all that many boots,
are there?

MOTHER COURAGE: Yvette, it's no time for checking your cart,
s'posing it is yours. You promised you'd talk to sergeant
about Swiss Cheese, there ain't a minute to lose, they say in
an hour he'll be courtmartialled.

YVETTE: Just let me count the shirts.

MOTHER COURAGE *pulling her down by the skirt*: You bloody
vampire. Swiss Cheese's life's at stake. And not a word about
who's making the offer, for God's sake, pretend it's your
friend, else we're all done for cause we looked after him.

YVETTE: I fixed to meet that one-eyed fellow in the copse, he
should be there by now.

THE CHAPLAIN: It doesn't have to be the whole two hundred
either, I'd go up to a hundred and fifty, that may be enough.

MOTHER COURAGE: Since when has it been your money? You
kindly keep out of this. You'll get your hotpot all right, don't
worry. Hurry up and don't haggle, it's life or death. *Pushes
Yvette off.*

THE CHAPLAIN: Far be it from me to interfere, but what are we
going to live on? You're saddled with a daughter who can't
earn her keep.

MOTHER COURAGE: I'm counting on regimental cash box, Mr
Clever. They'll allow it as his expenses.

THE CHAPLAIN: But will she get the message right?

MOTHER COURAGE: It's her interest I should spend her two
hundred so she gets the cart. She's set on that, God knows
how long that colonel of hers'll last. Kattrin, polish the
knives, there's the pumice. And you, stop hanging round like
Jesus on Mount of Olives, get moving, wash them glasses,
we'll have fifty or more of cavalry in tonight and I don't want
to hear a lot of 'I'm not accustomed to having to run about,
oh my poor feet, we never ran in church'. Thank the Lord
they're corruptible. After all, they ain't wolves, just humans
out for money. Corruption in humans is same as compassion
in God. Corruption's our only hope. Long as we have it
there'll be lenient sentences and even an innocent man'll have
a chance of being let off.

YVETTE *comes in panting*: They'll do it for two hundred. But it's got to be quick. Soon be out of their hands. Best thing is I go right away to my colonel with the one-eyed man. He's admitted he had the box, they put the thumbscrews on him. But he chucked it in the river soon as he saw they were on his track. The box is a write-off. I'll go and get the money from my colonel, shall I?

MOTHER COURAGE: Box is a write-off? How'm I to pay back two hundred then?

YVETTE: Oh, you thought you'd get it from the box, did you? And I was to be Joe Soap I suppose? Better not count on that. You'll have to pay up if you want Swiss Cheese back, or would you sooner I dropped the whole thing so's you can keep your cart?

MOTHER COURAGE: That's something I didn't allow for. Don't worry, you'll get your cart, I've said goodbye to it, had it seventeen years, I have. I just need a moment to think, it's bit sudden, what'm I to do, two hundred's too much for me, pity you didn't beat 'em down. Must keep a bit back, else any Tom, Dick and Harry'll be able to shove me in ditch. Go and tell them I'll pay hundred and twenty florins, else it's all off, either way I'm losing me cart.

YVETTE: They won't do it. That one-eyed man's impatient already, keeps looking over his shoulder, he's so worked up. Hadn't I best pay them the whole two hundred?

MOTHER COURAGE *in despair*: I can't pay that. Thirty years I been working. She's twenty-five already, and no husband. I got her to think of too. Don't push me, I know what I'm doing. Say a hundred and twenty, or it's off.

YVETTE: It's up to you. *Rushes off.*

*Without looking at either the chaplain or her daughter, Mother Courage sits down to help Kattrin polish knives.*

MOTHER COURAGE: Don't smash them glasses, they ain't ours now. Watch what you're doing, you'll cut yourself. Swiss Cheese'll be back, I'll pay two hundred if it comes to the pinch. You'll get your brother, love. For eighty florins we could fill a pack with goods and start again. Plenty of folk has to make do.

THE CHAPLAIN: The Lord will provide, it says.

MOTHER COURAGE: See they're properly dry. *She cleans knives in silence. Kattrin suddenly runs behind the cart, sobbing.*

YVETTE *comes running in*: They won't do it. I told you so. The one-eyed man wanted to leave right away, said there was no point. He says he's just waiting for the drum-roll; that means sentence has been pronounced. I offered a hundred and fifty. He didn't even blink. I had to convince him to stay there so's I could have another word with you.

MOTHER COURAGE: Tell him I'll pay the two hundred. Hurry! *Yvette runs off. They sit in silence. The chaplain has stopped polishing the glasses.* I reckon I bargained too long. *In the distance drumming is heard. The chaplain gets up and goes to the rear. Mother Courage remains seated. It grows dark. The drumming stops. It grows light once more. Mother Courage is sitting exactly as before.*

YVETTE *arrives, very pale*: Well, you got what you asked for, with your haggling and trying to keep your cart. Eleven bullets they gave him, that's all. You don't deserve I should bother any more about you. But I did hear they don't believe the box really is in the river. They've an idea it's here and anyhow that you're connected with him. They're going to bring him here, see if you gives yourself away when you sees him. Thought I'd better warn you so's you don't recognise him, else you'll all be for it. They're right on my heels, best tell you quick. Shall I keep Kattrin away? *Mother Courage shakes her head.* Does she know? She mayn't have heard the drumming or know what it meant.

MOTHER COURAGE: She knows. Get her.

*Yvette fetches Kattrin, who goes to her mother and stands beside her. Mother Courage takes her hand. Two lansequenets come carrying a stretcher with something lying on it covered by a sheet. The sergeant marches beside them. They set down the stretcher.*

SERGEANT: Here's somebody we dunno the name of. It's got to be listed, though, so everything's shipshape. He had a meal here. Have a look, see if you know him. *He removes the sheet.* Know him? *Mother Courage shakes her head.* What, never see him before he had that meal here? *Mother Courage shakes her head.* Pick him up. Chuck him in the pit. He's got nobody knows him. *They carry him away.*

# 4

## MOTHER COURAGE SINGS THE SONG OF THE GRAND CAPITULATION.

*Outside an officer's tent.*

*Mother Courage is waiting. A clerk looks out of the tent.*

THE CLERK: I know you. You had a paymaster from the Lutherans with you, what was in hiding. I'd not complain if I were you.

MOTHER COURAGE: But I got a complaint to make. I'm innocent, would look as how I'd a bad conscience if I let this pass. Slashed everything in me cart to pieces with their sabres, they did, then wanted I should pay five taler fine for nowt, I tell you, nowt.

THE CLERK: Take my tip, better shut up. We're short of canteens, so we let you go on trading, specially if you got a bad conscience and pay a fine now and then.

MOTHER COURAGE: I got a complaint.

THE CLERK: Have it your own way. Then you must wait till the captain's free. *Withdraws inside the tent.*

YOUNG SOLDIER *enters aggressively*: Bouque la Madonne! Where's that bleeding pig of a captain what's took my reward money to swig with his tarts? I'll do him.

OLDER SOLDIER *running after him*: Shut up. They'll put you in irons.

YOUNG SOLDIER: Out of there, you thief! I'll slice you into pork chops, I will. Pocketing my prize money after I'd swum the river, only one in the whole squadron, and now I can't even buy meself a beer. I'm not standing for that. Come on out there so I can cut you up!

OLDER SOLDIER: Blessed Mother of God, he's asking for trouble.

MOTHER COURAGE: Is it some reward he weren't paid?

YOUNG SOLDIER: Lemme go, I'll slash you too while I'm at it.

OLDER SOLDIER: He rescued the colonel's horse and got no reward for it. He's young yet, still wet behind the ears.

MOTHER COURAGE: Let him go, he ain't a dog you got to chain up. Wanting your reward is good sound sense. Why be a hero otherwise?

YOUNG SOLDIER: So's he can sit in there and booze. You're shit-scared, the lot of you. I done something special and I want my reward.

MOTHER COURAGE: Don't you shout at me, young fellow. Got me own worries, I have; any road you should spare your voice, be needing it when captain comes, else there he'll be and you too hoarse to make a sound, which'll make it hard for him to clap you in irons till you turn blue. People what shouts like that can't keep it up ever; half an hour, and they have to be rocked to sleep, they're so tired.

YOUNG SOLDIER: I ain't tired and to hell with sleep. I'm hungry. They make our bread from acorns and hemp-seed, and they even skimp on that. He's whoring away my reward and I'm hungry. I'll do him.

MOTHER COURAGE: Oh I see, you're hungry. Last year that general of yours ordered you all off roads and across fields so corn should be trampled flat; I could've got ten florins for a pair of boots s'pose I'd had boots and s'pose anyone'd been able to pay ten florins. Thought he'd be well away from that area this year, he did, but here he is, still there, and hunger is great. I see what you're angry about.

YOUNG SOLDIER: I won't have it, don't talk to me, it ain't fair and I'm not standing for that.

MOTHER COURAGE: And you're right; but how long? How long you not standing for unfairness? One hour, two hours? Didn't ask yourself that, did you, but it's the whole point, and why, once you're in irons it's too bad if you suddenly finds you can put up with unfairness after all.

YOUNG SOLDIER: What am I listening to you for, I'd like to know? Bouque la Madonne, where's that captain?

MOTHER COURAGE: You been listening to me because you knows it's like what I say, your anger has gone up in smoke already, it was just a short one and you needed a long one, but where you going to get it from?

YOUNG SOLDIER: Are you trying to tell me asking for my reward is wrong?

MOTHER COURAGE: Not a bit. I'm just telling you your anger ain't long enough, it's good for nowt, pity. If you'd a long one I'd be trying to prod you on. Cut him up, the swine, would be my advice to you in that case; but how about if you don't cut him up cause you feels your tail going between your legs? Then I'd look silly and captain'd take it out on me.

OLDER SOLDIER: You're perfectly right, he's just a bit crazy.

YOUNG SOLDIER: Very well, let's see if I don't cut him up. *Draws his sword.* When he arrives I'm going to cut him up.

THE CLERK *looks out*: The captain'll be here in one minute. Sit down.

*The young soldier sits down.*

MOTHER COURAGE: He's sitting now. See, what did I say? You're sitting now. Ah, how well they know us, no one need tell 'em how to go about it. Sit down! and, bingo, we're sitting. And sitting and sedition don't mix. Don't try to stand up, you won't stand the way you was standing before. I shouldn't worry about what I think; I'm no better, not one moment. Bought up all our fighting spirit, they have. Eh? S'pose I kick back, might be bad for business. Let me tell you a thing or two about the Grand Capitulation. *She sings the Song of the Grand Capitulation:*

Back when I was young, I was brought to realise
What a very special person I must be
(Not just any old cottager's daughter, what with my looks
    and my talents and my urge towards Higher Things)
And insisted that my soup should have no hairs in it.
No one makes a sucker out of me!

WESTCHESTER PUBLIC LIBRARY CHESTERTON, IN

(All or nothing, only the best is good enough, each man for
    himself, nobody's telling *me* what to do.)
Then I heard a tit
Chirp: Wait a bit!
    And you'll be marching with the band
    In step, responding to command
    And striking up your little dance:
    Now we advance.
    And now: parade, form square!
    Then men swear God's there—
    Not the faintest chance!

In no time at all anyone who looked could see
That I'd learned to take my medicine with good grace.
(Two kids on my hands and look at the price of bread, and
    things they expect of you!)
When they finally came to feel that they were through
    with me
They'd got me grovelling on my face.
(Takes all sorts to make a world, you scratch my back and I'll
    scratch yours, no good banging your head against a brick
    wall.)
Then I heard that tit
Chirp: Wait a bit!
    And you'll be marching with the band
    In step, responding to command
    And striking up your little dance:
    Now they advance.
    And now: parade, form square!
    Then men swear God's there—
    Not the faintest chance!

I've known people tried to storm the summits:
There's no star too bright or seems too far away.
(Dogged does it, where there's a will there's a way, by hook
    or by crook.)
As each peak disclosed fresh peaks to come, it's
Strange how much a plain straw hat could weigh.

(You have to cut your coat according to your cloth.)
Then I hear the tit
Chirp: Wait a bit!
   And they'll be marching with the band
   In step, responding to command
   And striking up their little dance:
   Now they advance
   And now: parade, form square!
   Then men swear God's there—
   Not the faintest chance!

MOTHER COURAGE *to the young soldier*: That's why I reckon
  you should stay there with your sword drawn if you're truly
  set on it and your anger's big enough, because you got
  grounds, I agree, but if your anger's a short one best leave
  right away.
YOUNG SOLDIER: Oh stuff it. *He staggers off with the older
  soldier following.*
THE CLERK *sticks his head out*: Captain's here now. You can
  make your complaint.
MOTHER COURAGE: I changed me mind. I ain't complaining.
  *Exit.*

# 5

TWO YEARS HAVE GONE BY. THE WAR IS SPREADING
TO NEW AREAS. CEASELESSLY ON THE MOVE,
COURAGE'S LITTLE CART CROSSES POLAND,
MORAVIA, BAVARIA, ITALY THEN BAVARIA AGAIN.
1631. TILLY'S VICTORY AT LEIPZIG COSTS
MOTHER COURAGE FOUR OFFICERS' SHIRTS.

*Mother Courage's cart has stopped in a badly shot-up village.*

*Thin military music in the distance. Two soldiers at the bar being served by Kattrin and Mother Courage. One of them has a lady's fur coat over his shoulders.*

MOTHER COURAGE: Can't pay, that it? No money, no schnapps. They give us victory parades, but catch them giving men their pay.

SOLDIER: I want my schnapps. I missed the looting. That double-crossing general only allowed an hour's looting in the town. He ain't an inhuman monster, he said. Town must of paid him.

THE CHAPLAIN *stumbles in*: There are people still lying in that yard. The peasant's family. Somebody give me a hand. I need linen.

*The second soldier goes off with him. Kattrin becomes very excited and tries to make her mother produce linen.*

MOTHER COURAGE: I got none. All my bandages was sold to regiment. I ain't tearing up my officer's shirts for that lot.

THE CHAPLAIN *calling back*: I need linen, I tell you.

MOTHER COURAGE *blocking Kattrin's way into the cart by sitting on the step*: I'm giving nowt. They'll never pay, and why, nowt to pay with.

THE CHAPLAIN *bending over a woman he has carried in*: Why d'you stay around during the gunfire?

PEASANT WOMAN *feebly*: Farm.

MOTHER COURAGE: Catch them abandoning anything. But now I'm s'posed to foot the bill. I won't do it.

FIRST SOLDIER: Those are Protestants. What they have to be Protestants for?

MOTHER COURAGE: They ain't bothering about faith. They lost their farm.

SECOND SOLDIER: They're no Protestants. They're Catholics like us.

FIRST SOLDIER: No way of sorting 'em out in a bombardment.

A PEASANT *brought in by the chaplain*: My arm's gone.

THE CHAPLAIN: Where's that linen?

MOTHER COURAGE: I can't give nowt. What with expenses, taxes, loan interest and bribes. *Making guttural noises, Kattrin raises a plank and threatens her mother with it.* You gone plain crazy? Put that plank away or I'll paste you one, you cow. I'm giving nowt, don't want to, got to think of meself. *The chaplain lifts her off the steps and sets her on the ground, then starts pulling out shirts and tearing them into strips.* My officers' shirts! Half a florin apiece! I'm ruined. *From the house comes the cry of a child in pain.*

THE PEASANT: The baby's in there still. *Kattrin dashes in.*

THE CHAPLAIN *to the woman*: Don't move. They'll get it out.

MOTHER COURAGE: Stop her, roof may fall in.

THE CHAPLAIN: I'm not going back in there.

MOTHER COURAGE *torn both ways*: Don't waste my precious linen.

*Kattrin brings a baby out of the ruins.*

MOTHER COURAGE: How nice, found another baby to cart around? Give it to its ma this instant, unless you'd have me fighting for hours to get it off you, like last time, d'you hear? *To the second soldier*: Don't stand there gawping, you go back and tell them cut out that music, we can see it's a victory with our own eyes. All your victories mean to me is losses.

THE CHAPLAIN *tying a bandage*: Blood's coming through.

*Kattrin is rocking the baby and making lullaby noises.*

MOTHER COURAGE: Look at her, happy as a queen in all this misery; give it back at once, its mother's coming round. *She catches the first soldier, who has been attacking the drinks and is trying to make off with one of the bottles.* Psia krew! Thought you'd score another victory, you animal? Now pay.

FIRST SOLDIER: I got nowt.

MOTHER COURAGE *pulling the fur coat off his back*: Then leave that coat, it's stolen any road.

THE CHAPLAIN: There's still someone under there.

OUTSIDE THE BAVARIAN TOWN OF INGOLSTADT
COURAGE PARTICIPATES IN THE FUNERAL OF THE
LATE IMPERIAL COMMANDER TILLY. DISCUSSIONS
ARE HELD ABOUT WAR HEROES AND THE WAR'S
DURATION. THE CHAPLAIN COMPLAINS THAT HIS
TALENTS ARE LYING FALLOW AND DUMB KATTRIN
GETS THE RED BOOTS. THE YEAR IS 1632.

*Inside a canteen tent.*

*It has a bar towards the rear. Rain. Sound of drums and funeral
music. The chaplain and the regimental clerk are playing a
board game. Mother Courage and her daughter are stocktaking.*

THE CHAPLAIN: Now the funeral procession will be moving
off.

MOTHER COURAGE: Too bad about commander in chief—
twenty-two pairs those socks—he fell by accident, they say.
Mist over fields, that was the trouble. General had just been
haranguing a regiment saying they must fight to last man
and last round, he was riding back when mist made him
lose direction so he was up front and a bullet got him in
midst of battle—only four hurricane lamps left. *A whistle
from the rear. She goes to the bar.* You scrimshankers, dodging your commander in chief's funeral, scandal I call it.
*Pours drinks.*

THE CLERK: They should never of paid troops out before the
funeral. Instead of going now they're all getting pissed.

THE CHAPLAIN *to the clerk*: Aren't you supposed to go to the
funeral?

THE CLERK: Dodged it cause of the rain.

MOTHER COURAGE: It's different with you, your uniform might get wet. I heard they wanted to toll bells for the funeral as usual, except it turned out all churches had been blown to smithereens by his orders, so poor old commander in chief won't be hearing no bells as they let the coffin down. They're going to let off three salvoes instead to cheer things up—seventeen belts.

SHOUTS *from the bar*: Hey, missis, a brandy!

MOTHER COURAGE: Let's see your money. No, I ain't having you in my tent with your disgusting boots. You can drink outside, rain or no rain. *To the clerk:* I'm only letting in sergeants and up. Commander in chief had been having his worries, they say. S'posed to have been trouble with Second Regiment cause he stopped their pay, said it was a war of faith and they should do it for free. *Funeral march. All look to the rear.*

THE CHAPLAIN: Now they'll be filing past the noble corpse.

MOTHER COURAGE: Can't help feeling sorry for those generals and emperors, there they are maybe thinking they're doing something extra special what folk'll talk about in years to come, and earning a public monument, like conquering the world for instance, that's a fine ambition for a general, how's he to know any better? I mean, he plagues hisself to death, then it all breaks down on account of ordinary folk what just wants their beer and bit of a chat, nowt higher. Finest plans get bolloxed up by the pettiness of them as should be carrying them out, because emperors can't do nowt themselves, they just counts on soldiers and people to back 'em up whatever happens, am I right?

THE CHAPLAIN *laughs*: Courage, you're right, aside from the soldiers. They do their best. Give me that lot outside there, for instance, drinking their brandy in the rain, and I'd guarantee to make you one war after another for a hundred years if need be, and I'm no trained general.

MOTHER COURAGE: You don't think war might end, then?

THE CHAPLAIN: What, because the commander in chief's gone? Don't be childish. They're two a penny, no shortage of heroes.

MOTHER COURAGE: Ee, I'm not asking for fun of it, but because I'm thinking whether to stock up, prices are low now,
but if war's going to end it's money down the drain.

THE CHAPLAIN: I realise it's a serious question. There've always been people going round saying 'the war can't go on for
ever'. I tell you there's nothing to stop it going on for ever. Of
course there can be a bit of a breathing space. The war may
need to get its second wind, it may even have an accident so
to speak. There's no guarantee against that; nothing's perfect
on this earth of ours. A perfect war, the sort you might say
couldn't be improved on, that's something we shall probably
never see. It can suddenly come to a standstill for some quite
unforeseen reason, you can't allow for everything. A slight
case of negligence, and it's bogged down up to the axles. And
then it's a matter of hauling the war out of the mud again.
But emperor and kings and popes will come to its rescue. So
on the whole it has nothing serious to worry about, and will
live to a ripe old age.

A SOLDIER sings at the bar:

> A schnapps, landlord, you're late!
> A soldier cannot wait
> To do his emperor's orders.

Make it a double, this is a holiday.

MOTHER COURAGE: S'pose I went by what you say . . .

THE CHAPLAIN: Think it out for yourself. What's to compete
with the war?

THE SOLDIER at the rear:

> Your breast, my girl, you're late!
> A soldier cannot wait
> To ride across the borders.

THE CLERK unexpectedly: And what about peace? I'm from
Bohemia and I'd like to go home some day.

THE CHAPLAIN: Would you indeed? Ah, peace. Where is the
hole once the cheese has been eaten?
THE SOLDIER *at the rear*:

> Lead trumps, my friend, you're late!
> A soldier cannot wait.
> His emperor needs him badly.
>
> Your blessing, priest, you're late!
> A soldier cannot wait.
> Must lay his life down gladly.

THE CLERK: In the long run life's impossible if there's no peace.
THE CHAPLAIN: I'd say there's peace in war too; it has its peaceful moments. Because war satisfies all requirements, peaceable
ones included, they're catered for, and it would simply fizzle
out if they weren't. In war you can do a crap like in the depths
of peacetime, then between one battle and the next you can
have a beer, then even when you're moving up you can lay your
head on your arms and have a bit of shuteye in the ditch, it's
entirely possible. During a charge you can't play cards maybe,
but nor can you in the depths of peacetime when you're
ploughing, and after a victory there are various openings. You
may get a leg blown off, then you start by making a lot of fuss
as though it were serious, but afterwards you calm down or get
given a schnapps, and you end up hopping around and the
war's no worse off than before. And what's to stop you being
fruitful and multiplying in the middle of all the butchery, behind a barn or something, in the long run you can't be held
back from it, and then the war will have your progeny and can
use them to carry on with. No, the war will always find an out-
let, mark my words. Why should it ever stop?
*Kattrin has ceased working and is staring at the chaplain.*
MOTHER COURAGE: I'll buy fresh stock then. If you say so.
*Kattrin suddenly flings a basket full of bottles to the ground
and runs off.* Kattrin! *Laughs.* Damn me if she weren't waiting for peace. I promised her she'd get a husband soon as
peace came. *Hurries after her.*

THE CLERK *standing up*: I won. You been talking too much. Pay up.

MOTHER COURAGE *returning with Kattrin*: Don't be silly, war'll go on a bit longer, and we'll make a bit more money, and peacetime'll be all the nicer for it. Now you go into town, that's ten minutes' walk at most, fetch things from Golden Lion, the expensive ones, we can fetch the rest in cart later, it's all arranged, regimental clerk here will go with you. Nearly everybody's attending commander in chief's funeral, nowt can happen to you. Careful now, don't let them steal nowt, think of your dowry.

*Kattrin puts a cloth over her head and leaves with the clerk.*

THE CHAPLAIN: Is that all right to let her go with the clerk?

MOTHER COURAGE: She's not that pretty they'd want to ruin her.

THE CHAPLAIN: I admire the way you run your business and always win through. I see why they called you Courage.

MOTHER COURAGE: Poor folk got to have courage. Why, they're lost. Simply getting up in morning takes some doing in their situation. Or ploughing a field, and in a war at that. Mere fact they bring kids into world shows they got courage, 'cause there's no hope for them. They have to hang one another and slaughter one another, so just looking each other in face must call for courage. Being able to put up with emperor and pope shows supernatural courage, 'cause those two cost 'em their lives. *She sits down, takes a little pipe from her purse and smokes.* You might chop us a bit of kindling.

THE CHAPLAIN *reluctantly removing his coat and preparing to chop up sticks*: I happen to be a pastor of souls, not a wood-cutter.

MOTHER COURAGE: I got no soul, you see. Need firewood, though.

THE CHAPLAIN: Where's that stumpy pipe from?

MOTHER COURAGE: Just a pipe.

THE CHAPLAIN: What d'you mean, 'just', it's a quite particular pipe, that.

MOTHER COURAGE: Aha?

THE CHAPLAIN: That stumpy pipe belongs to the Oxenstierna Regiment's cook.

MOTHER COURAGE: If you know that already why ask, Mr Clever?

THE CHAPLAIN: Because I didn't know if you were aware what you're smoking. You might just have been rummaging around in your things, come across some old pipe or other, and used it out of sheer absence of mind.

MOTHER COURAGE: And why not?

THE CHAPLAIN: Because you didn't. You're smoking that deliberately.

MOTHER COURAGE: And why shouldn't I?

THE CHAPLAIN: Courage, I'm warning you. It's my duty. Probably you'll never clap eyes on the gentleman again, and that's no loss but your good fortune. He didn't make at all a reliable impression on me. Quite the opposite.

MOTHER COURAGE: Really? Nice fellow that.

THE CHAPLAIN: So he's what you would call a nice fellow? I wouldn't. Far be it from me to bear him the least ill-will, but nice is not what I would call him. More like one of those Don Juans, a slippery one. Have a look at that pipe if you don't believe me. You must admit it tells you a good deal about his character.

MOTHER COURAGE: Nowt that I can see. Worn out, I'd call it.

THE CHAPLAIN: Practically bitten through, you mean. A man of wrath. That is the pipe of an unscrupulous man of wrath; you must see that if you have any discrimination left.

MOTHER COURAGE: Don't chop my chopping block in two.

THE CHAPLAIN: I told you I'm not a woodcutter by trade. I studied to be a pastor of souls. My talent and abilities are being abused in this place, by manual labour. My God-given endowments are denied expression. It's a sin. You have never heard me preach. One sermon of mine can put a regiment in such a frame of mind it'll treat the enemy like a flock of sheep. Life to them is a smelly old foot-cloth which they fling away in a vision of final victory. God has given me the gift of speech. I can preach so you'll lose all sense of sight and hearing.

MOTHER COURAGE: I don't wish to lose my sense of sight and hearing. Where'd that leave me?

THE CHAPLAIN: Courage, I have often thought that your dry way of talking conceals more that just a warm heart. You too are human and need warmth.

MOTHER COURAGE: Best way for us to get this tent warm is have plenty of firewood.

THE CHAPLAIN: Don't change the subject. Seriously, Courage, I sometimes ask myself what it would be like if our relationship were to become somewhat closer. I mean, given that the whirlwind of war has so strangely whirled us together.

MOTHER COURAGE: I'd say it was close enough. I cook meals for you and you run around and chop firewood for instance.

THE CHAPLAIN *coming closer*: You know what I mean by closer; it's not a relationship founded on meals and wood-chopping and other such base necessities. Let your head speak, harden thyself not.

MOTHER COURAGE: Don't you come at me with that axe. That'd be too close a relationship.

THE CHAPLAIN: You shouldn't make a joke of it. I'm a serious person and I've thought about what I'm saying.

MOTHER COURAGE: Be sensible, padre. I like you. I don't want to row you. All I'm after is get myself and children through all this with my cart. I don't see it as mine, and I ain't in the mood for private affairs. Right now I'm taking a gamble, buying stores just when commander in chief's fallen and all the talk's of peace. Where d'you reckon you'd turn if I'm ruined? Don't know, do you? You chop us some kindling wood, then we can keep warm at night, that's quite something these times. What's this? *She gets up. Enter Kattrin, out of breath, with a wound above her eye. She is carrying a variety of stuff: parcels, leather goods, a drum and so on.*

MOTHER COURAGE: What happened, someone assault you? On your way back? She was assaulted on her way back. Bet it was that trooper was getting drunk here. I shouldn't have let you go, love. Drop that stuff. Not too bad, just a flesh wound you got. I'll bandage it and in a week it'll be all right. Worse than wild beasts, they are. *She ties up the wound.*

THE CHAPLAIN: It's not them I blame. They never went raping back home. The fault lies with those that start wars, it brings humanity's lowest instincts to the surface.

MOTHER COURAGE: Calm down. Didn't clerk come back with you? That's because you're respectable, they don't bother. Wound ain't a deep one, won't leave no mark. There you are, all bandaged up. You'll get something, love, keep calm. Something I put aside for you, wait till you see. *She delves into a sack and brings out Yvette's red high-heeled boots.* Made you open your eyes, eh? Something you always wanted. They're yours. Put 'em on quick, before I change me mind. Won't leave no mark, and what if it does? Ones I'm really sorry for's the ones they fancy. Drag them around till they're worn out, they do. Those they don't care for they leaves alive. I seen girls before now had pretty faces, then in no time looking fit to frighten a hyaena. Can't even go behind a bush without risking touble, horrible life they lead. Same like with trees, straight well-shaped ones get chopped down to make beams for houses and crooked ones live happily ever after. So it's a stroke of luck for you really. Them boots'll be all right, I greased them before putting them away.

*Kattrin leaves the boots where they are and crawls into the cart.*

THE CHAPLAIN: Let's hope she's not disfigured.

MOTHER COURAGE: She'll have a scar. No use her waiting for peacetime now.

THE CHAPLAIN: She didn't let them steal the things.

MOTHER COURAGE: Maybe I shouldn't have dinned that into her so. Wish I knew what went on in that head of hers. Just once she stayed out all night, once in all those years. Afterwards she went around like before, except she worked harder. Couldn't get her to tell what had happened. Worried me quite a while, that did. *She collects the articles brought by Kattrin, and sorts them angrily.* That's war for you. Nice way to get a living!

*Sound of cannon fire.*

THE CHAPLAIN: Now they'll be burying the commander in chief. This is a historic moment.

MOTHER COURAGE: What I call a historic moment is them bashing my daughter over the eye. She's half wrecked already, won't get no husband now, and her so crazy about kids; any road she's only dumb from war, soldier stuffed something in her mouth when she was little. As for Swiss Cheese I'll never see him again, and where Eilif is God alone knows. War be damned.

# 7

## MOTHER COURAGE AT THE PEAK OF HER BUSINESS CAREER.

*High road.*

*The chaplain, Mother Courage and Kattrin are pulling the cart, which is hung with new wares. Mother Courage is wearing a necklace of silver coins.*

MOTHER COURAGE: I won't have you folk spoiling my war for me. I'm told it kills off the weak, but they're write-off in peacetime too. And war gives its people a better deal.
*She sings:*

> And if you feel your forces fading
> You won't be there to share the fruits.
> But what is war but private trading
> That deals in blood instead of boots?

And what's the use of settling down? Them as does are first to go. *Sings:*

> Some people think to live by looting
> The goods some others haven't got.
> You think it's just a line they're shooting
> Until you hear they have been shot.
>
> And some I saw dig six feet under
> In haste to lie down and pass out.
> Now they're at rest perhaps they wonder
> Just what was all their haste about.

*They pull it further.*

# 8

THE SAME YEAR SEES THE DEATH OF THE SWEDISH
KING GUSTAVUS ADOLPHUS AT THE BATTLE OF
LÜTZEN. PEACE THREATENS TO RUIN MOTHER
COURAGE'S BUSINESS. COURAGE'S DASHING SON
PERFORMS ONE HEROIC DEED TOO MANY
AND COMES TO A STICKY END.

*Camp.*

*A summer morning. In front of the cart stand an old woman
and her son. The son carries a large sack of bedding.*

MOTHER COURAGE'S VOICE *from inside the cart*: Does it need
to be this ungodly hour?

THE YOUNG MAN: We walked twenty miles in the night and
got to be back today.

MOTHER COURAGE'S VOICE: What am I to do with bedding?
Folk've got no houses.

THE YOUNG MAN: Best have a look first.

THE OLD WOMAN: This place is no good either. Come on.

THE YOUNG MAN: What, and have them sell the roof over our
head for taxes? She might pay three florins if you throw in
the bracelet. *Bells start ringing.* Listen, mother.

VOICES *from the rear*: Peace! Swedish king's been killed.

MOTHER COURAGE *sticks her head out of the cart. She has not
yet done her hair*: What's that bell-ringing about in mid-week?

THE CHAPLAIN *crawling out from under the cart*: What are
they shouting? Peace?

MOTHER COURAGE: Don't tell me peace has broken out just
after I laid in new stock.

THE CHAPLAIN *calling to the rear*: That true? Peace?

VOICES: Three weeks ago, they say, only no one told us.

THE CHAPLAIN *to Courage*: What else would they be ringing the bells for?

VOICES: A whole lot of Lutherans have driven into town, they brought the news.

THE YOUNG MAN: Mother, it's peace. What's the matter? *The old woman has collapsed.*

MOTHER COURAGE *speaking into the cart*: Holy cow! Kattrin, peace! Put your black dress on, we're going to church. Least we can do for Swiss Cheese. Is it true, though?

THE YOUNG MAN: The people here say so. They've made peace. Can you get up? *The old woman stands up dumbfounded.* I'll get the saddlery going again, I promise. It'll all work out. Father will get his bedding back. Can you walk? *To the chaplain:* She came over queer. It's the news. She never thought there'd be peace again. Father always said so. We're going straight home. *They go off.*

MOTHER COURAGE'S VOICE: Give her a schnapps.

THE CHAPLAIN: They've already gone.

MOTHER COURAGE'S VOICE: What's up in camp?

THE CHAPLAIN: They're assembling. I'll go on over. Shouldn't I put on my clerical garb?

MOTHER COURAGE'S VOICE: Best check up before parading yourself as heretic. I'm glad about peace, never mind if I'm ruined. Any road I'll have got two of my children through the war. Be seeing Eilif again now.

THE CHAPLAIN: And who's that walking down the lines? Bless me, the army commander's cook.

THE COOK *somewhat bedraggled and carrying a bundle*: What do I behold? The padre!

THE CHAPLAIN: Courage, we've got company.
*Mother Courage clambers out.*

THE COOK: I promised I'd drop over for a little talk soon as I had the time. I've not forgotten your brandy, Mrs Fierling.

MOTHER COURAGE: Good grief, the general's cook! After all these years! Where's my eldest boy Eilif?

THE COOK: Hasn't he got here? He left before me, he was on his way to see you too.

THE CHAPLAIN: I shall don my clerical garb, just a moment.

*Goes off behind the cart.*

MOTHER COURAGE: Then he may be here any minute. *Calls into the cart:* Kattrin, Eilif's on his way. Get cook a glass of brandy, Kattrin! *Kattrin does not appear.* Drag your hair down over it, that's all right. Mr Lamb's no stranger. *Fetches the brandy herself.* She don't like to come out, peace means nowt to her. Took too long coming, it did. They gave her a crack over one eye, you barely notice it now but she thinks folks are staring at her.

THE COOK: Ah yes. War. *He and Mother Courage sit down.*

MOTHER COURAGE: Cooky, you caught me at a bad moment. I'm ruined.

THE COOK: What? That's hard.

MOTHER COURAGE: Peace'll wring my neck. I went and took Chaplain's advice, laid in fresh stocks only t'other day. And now they're going to demobilise and I'll be left sitting on me wares.

THE COOK: What d'you want to go and listen to padre for? If I hadn't been in such a hurry that time, the Catholics arriving so quickly and all, I'd warned you against that man. All piss and wind, he is. So he's the authority around here, eh?

MOTHER COURAGE: He's been doing washing-up for me and helping pull.

THE COOK: Him pull! I bet he told you some of those jokes of his too, I know him, got a very unhealthy view of women, he has, all my good influence on him went for nowt. He ain't steady.

MOTHER COURAGE: You steady then?

THE COOK: Whatever else I ain't, I'm steady. Mud in your eye!

MOTHER COURAGE: Steady, that's nowt. I only had one steady fellow, thank God. Hardest I ever had to work in me life; he flogged the kids' blankets soon as autumn came, and he called me mouth-organ an unchristian instrument. Ask me, you ain't saying much for yourself admitting you're steady.

THE COOK: Still tough as nails, I see; but that's what I like about you.

MOTHER COURAGE: Now don't tell me you been dreaming of me nails.

THE COOK: Well, well, here we are, along with armistice bells and your brandy like what nobody else ever serves, it's famous, that is.

MOTHER COURAGE: I don't give two pins for your armistice bells just now. Can't see 'em handing out all the back pay what's owing, so where does that leave me with my famous brandy? Had your pay yet?

THE COOK *hesitantly*: Not exactly. That's why we all shoved off. If that's how it is, I thought, I'll go and visit friends. So here I am sitting with you.

MOTHER COURAGE: Other words you got nowt.

THE COOK: High time they stopped that bloody clanging. Wouldn't mind getting into some sort of trade. I'm fed up being cook to that lot. I'm s'posed to rustle them up meals out of tree roots and old bootsoles, then they fling the hot soup in my face. Cook these days is a dog's life. Sooner do war service, only of course it's peacetime now. *He sees the chaplain reappearing in his old garments.* More about that later.

THE CHAPLAIN: It's still all right, only had a few moths in it.

THE COOK: Can't see why you bother. You won't get your old job back, who are you to inspire now to earn his pay honourably and lay down his life? What's more I got a bone to pick with you, cause you advised this lady to buy a lot of unnecessary goods saying war would go on for ever.

THE CHAPLAIN *heatedly*: I'd like to know what concern that is of yours.

THE COOK: Because it's unscrupulous, that sort of thing is. How dare you meddle in other folks' business arrangements with your unwanted advice?

THE CHAPLAIN: Who's meddling? *To Courage:* I never knew this gentleman was such an intimate you had to account to him for everything.

MOTHER COURAGE: Keep your hair on, cook's only giving his personal opinion and you can't deny your war was a flop.

THE CHAPLAIN: You should not blaspheme against peace, Courage. You are a hyaena of the battlefield.

MOTHER COURAGE: I'm what?

THE COOK: If you're going to insult this lady you'll have to settle with me.

THE CHAPLAIN: It's not you I'm talking to. Your intentions are
only too transparent. *To Courage:* But when I see you picking up peace betwixt your finger and your thumb like some
dirty old snot-rag, then my humanity feels outraged; for then
I see that you don't want peace but war, because you profit
from it; in which case you shouldn't forget the ancient saying
that whosoever sups with the devil needs a long spoon.

MOTHER COURAGE: I got no use for war, and war ain't got
much use for me. But I'm not being called no hyaena, you
and me's through.

THE CHAPLAIN: Then why grumble about peace when everybody's breathing sighs of relief? Because of some old junk in
your cart?

MOTHER COURAGE: My goods ain't old junk but what I lives
by, and you too up to now.

THE CHAPLAIN: Off war, in other words. Aha.

THE COOK *to the chaplain:* You're old enough to know it's always a mistake offering advice. *To Courage:* Way things are,
your best bet's to get rid of certain goods quick as you can
before prices hit rock-bottom. Dress yourself and get moving, not a moment to lose.

MOTHER COURAGE: That ain't bad advice. I'll do that, I guess.

THE CHAPLAIN: Because cooky says it.

MOTHER COURAGE: Why couldn't you say it? He's right, I'd
best go off to market. *Goes inside the cart.*

THE COOK: That's one to me, padre. You got no presence of
mind. What you should of said was: what, me offer advice,
all I done was discuss politics. Better not take me on. Cock-
fighting don't suit that get-up.

THE CHAPLAIN: If you don't stop your gob I'll murder you,
get-up or no get-up.

THE COOK *pulling off his boots and unwrapping his foot-
cloths:* Pity the war made such a godless shit of you, else
you'd easily get another parsonage now it's peacetime. Cooks
won't be needed, there's nowt to cook, but faith goes on just
the same, nowt changed in that direction.

THE CHAPLAIN: Mr Lamb, I'm asking you not to elbow me out. Since I came down in the world I've become a better person. I couldn't preach to anyone now.

*Enter Yvette Pottier in black, dressed up to the nines, carrying a cane. She is much older and fatter, and heavily powdered. She is followed by a manservant.*

YVETTE: Hullo there, everybody. Is this Mother Courage's establishment?

THE CHAPLAIN: It is. And with whom have we the honour . . . ?

YVETTE: With the Countess Starhemberg, my good man. Where's Courage?

THE CHAPLAIN *calls into the cart*: The Countess Starhemberg wishes to speak to you.

MOTHER COURAGE'S VOICE: Just coming.

YVETTE: It's Yvette.

MOTHER COURAGE'S VOICE: Oh, Yvette!

YVETTE: Come to see how you are. *Sees the cook turn round aghast*: Pieter!

THE COOK: Yvette!

YVETTE: Well I never! How d'you come to be here?

THE COOK: Got a lift.

THE CHAPLAIN: You know each other then? Intimately?

YVETTE: I should think so. *She looks the cook over*. Fat.

THE COOK: Not all that skinny yourself.

YVETTE: All the same I'm glad to see you, you shit. Gives me a chance to say what I think of you.

THE CHAPLAIN: You say it, in full; but don't start till Courage is out here.

MOTHER COURAGE *coming out with all kinds of goods*: Yvette! *They embrace*. But what are you in mourning for?

YVETTE: Suits me, don't it? My husband the colonel died a few years back.

MOTHER COURAGE: That old fellow what nearly bought the cart?

YVETTE: His elder brother.

MOTHER COURAGE: Then you're sitting pretty. Nice to find somebody what's made it in this war.

YVETTE: Up and down and up again, that's the way it went.

MOTHER COURAGE: I'm not hearing a word against colonels, they make a mint of money.

THE CHAPLAIN: I would put my boots back on if I were you. *To Yvette:* You promised you would say what you think of the gentleman.

THE COOK: Don't kick up a stink here, Yvette.

MOTHER COURAGE: Yvette, this is a friend of mine.

YVETTE: That's old Puffing Piet.

THE COOK: Let's drop the nicknames. I'm called Lamb.

MOTHER COURAGE *laughs*: Puffing Piet! Him as made all the women crazy! Here, I been looking after your pipe for you.

THE CHAPLAIN: Smoking it, too.

YVETTE: What luck I can warn you against him. Worst of the lot, he was, rampaging along the whole Flanders coastline. Got more girls in trouble than he has fingers.

THE COOK: That's all a long while ago. Tain't true anyhow.

YVETTE: Stand up when a lady brings you into the conversation! How I loved this man! All the time he had a little dark girl with bandy legs, got her in trouble too of course.

THE COOK: Got you into high society more like, far as I can see.

YVETTE: Shut your trap, you pathetic remnant! Better watch out for him, though; fellows like that are still dangerous even when on their last legs.

MOTHER COURAGE *to Yvette*: Come along, got to get rid of my stuff afore prices start dropping. You might be able to put a word in for me at regiment, with your connections. *Calls into the cart:* Kattrin, church is off, I'm going to market instead. When Eilif turns up, one of you give him a drink. *Exit with Yvette.*

YVETTE *as she leaves*: Fancy a creature like that ever making me leave the straight and narrow path. Thank my lucky stars I managed to reach the top all the same. But I've cooked your goose, Puffing Piet, and that's something that'll be credited to me one day in the world to come.

THE CHAPLAIN: I would like to take as a text for our little talk 'The mills of God grind slowly'. Weren't you complaining about my jokes?

THE COOK: Dead out of luck, I am. It's like this, you see: I thought I might get a hot meal. Here am I starving, and now they'll be talking about me and she'll get quite a wrong picture. I think I'll clear out before she's back.

THE CHAPLAIN: I think so too.

THE COOK: Padre, I'm fed up already with this bloody peace. Human race has to go through fire and sword cause it's sinful from the cradle up. I wish I could be roasting a fat capon once again for the general, wherever he's got to, in mustard sauce with a carrot or two.

THE CHAPLAIN: Red cabbage. Red cabbage for a capon.

THE COOK: You're right, but carrots was what he had to have.

THE CHAPLAIN: No sense of what's fitting.

THE COOK: Not that it stopped you guzzling your share.

THE CHAPLAIN: With misgivings.

THE COOK: Anyway you must admit those were the days.

THE CHAPLAIN: I might admit it if pressed.

THE COOK: Now you've called her a hyaena your days here are finished. What you staring at?

THE CHAPLAIN: Eilif! *Eilif arrives, followed by soldiers with pikes. His hands are fettered. His face is chalky-white.* What's wrong?

EILIF: Where's mother?

THE CHAPLAIN: Gone into town.

EILIF: I heard she was around. They've allowed me to come and see her.

THE COOK *to the soldiers*: What you doing with him?

A SOLDIER: Something not nice.

THE CHAPLAIN: What's he been up to?

THE SOLDIER: Broke into a peasant's place. The wife's dead.

THE CHAPLAIN: How could you do a thing like that?

EILIF: It's what I did last time, ain't it?

THE COOK: Aye, but it's peace now.

EILIF: Shut up. All right if I sit down till she comes?

THE SOLDIER: We've no time.

THE CHAPLAIN: In wartime they recommended him for that, sat him at the general's right hand. Dashing, it was, in those days. Any chance of a word with the provost-marshal?

THE SOLDIER: Wouldn't do no good. Taking some peasant's cattle, what's dashing about that?

THE COOK: Dumb, I call it.

EILIF: If I'd been dumb you'd of starved, clever bugger.

THE COOK: But as you were clever you're going to be shot.

THE CHAPLAIN: We'd better fetch Kattrin out anyhow.

EILIF: Sooner have a glass of schnapps, could do with that.

THE SOLDIER: No time, come along.

THE CHAPLAIN: And what shall we tell your mother?

EILIF: Tell her it wasn't any different, tell her it was the same thing. Or tell her nowt. *The soldiers propel him away.*

THE CHAPLAIN: I'll accompany you on your grievous journey.

EILIF: Don't need any bloody parsons.

THE CHAPLAIN: Wait and see. *Follows him.*

THE COOK *calls after them*: I'll have to tell her, she'll want to see him.

THE CHAPLAIN: I wouldn't tell her anything. At most that he was here and will come again, maybe tomorrow. By then I'll be back and can break it to her. *Hurries off.*
*The cook looks after him, shaking his head, then walks restlessly around. Finally he comes up to the cart.*

THE COOK: Hoy! Don't you want to come out? I can understand you hiding away from peace. Like to do the same myself. Remember me, I'm general's cook? I was wondering if you'd a bit of something to eat while I wait for your mum. I don't half feel like a bit of pork, or bread even, just to fill the time. *Peers inside.* Head under blanket. *Sound of gunfire off.*

MOTHER COURAGE *runs in, out of breath and with all her goods still*: Cooky, peacetime's over. War's been on again three days now. Heard news before selling me stuff, thank God. They're having a shooting match with Lutherans in town. We must get the cart away at once. Kattrin, pack up! What you in the dumps for? What's wrong?

THE COOK: Nowt.

MOTHER COURAGE: Something is. I see it way you look.

THE COOK: 'Cause war's starting up again, I s'pose. Looks as if it'll be tomorrow night before I get next hot food inside me.

MOTHER COURAGE: You're lying, cooky.

THE COOK: Eilif was here. Had to leave almost at once, though.

MOTHER COURAGE: Was he now? Then we'll be seeing him on march. I'm joining our side this time. How's he look?

THE COOK: Same as usual.

MOTHER COURAGE: Oh, he'll never change. Take more than war to steal him from me. Clever, he is. You going to help me get packed? *Begins to pack up.* What's his news? Still in general's good books? Say anything about his deeds of valour?

THE COOK *glumly*: Repeated one of them, I'm told.

MOTHER COURAGE: Tell it me later, we got to move off. *Kattrin appears.* Kattrin, peacetime's finished now. We're moving on. *To the cook:* How about you?

THE COOK: Have to join up again.

MOTHER COURAGE: Why don't you . . . Where's padre?

THE COOK: Went into town with Eilif.

MOTHER COURAGE: Then you come along with us a way. Need somebody to help me.

THE COOK: That business with Yvette, you know . . .

MOTHER COURAGE: Done you no harm in my eyes. Opposite. Where there's smoke there's fire, they say. You coming along?

THE COOK: I won't say no.

MOTHER COURAGE: The Twelfth moved off already. Take the shaft. Here's a bit of bread. We must get round behind to Lutherans. Might even be seeing Eilif tonight. He's my favourite one. Short peace, wasn't it? Now we're off again. *She sings as the cook and Kattrin harness themselves up:*

> From Ulm to Metz, from Metz to Munich
> Courage will see the war gets fed.
> The war will show a well-filled tunic
> Given its daily shot of lead.
> But lead alone can hardly nourish
> It must have soldiers to subsist.
> It's you it needs to make it flourish.
> The war's still hungry. So enlist!

# 9

IT IS THE SEVENTEENTH YEAR OF THE GREAT WAR
OF FAITH. GERMANY HAS LOST MORE THAN HALF
HER INHABITANTS. THOSE WHO SURVIVE THE
BLOODBATH ARE KILLED OFF BY TERRIBLE
EPIDEMICS. ONCE-FERTILE AREAS ARE RAVAGED
BY FAMINE, WOLVES ROAM THE BURNT-OUT TOWNS.
IN AUTUMN 1634 WE FIND COURAGE IN THE
FICHTELGEBIRGE, OFF THE MAIN AXIS OF THE
SWEDISH ARMIES. THE WINTER THIS YEAR IS EARLY
AND HARSH. BUSINESS IS BAD, SO THAT THERE
IS NOTHING TO DO BUT BEG. THE COOK GETS A
LETTER FROM UTRECHT AND IS SENT PACKING.

*Outside a semi-dilapidated parsonage.*

*Grey morning in early winter. Gusts of wind. Mother Courage
and the cook in shabby sheepskins, drawing the cart.*

THE COOK: It's all dark, nobody up yet.
MOTHER COURAGE: Except it's parson's house. Have to crawl
out of bed to ring bells. Then he'll have hot soup.
THE COOK: What from when the whole village is burnt, we
seen it.
MOTHER COURAGE: It's lived in, though, dog was barking.
THE COOK: S'pose parson's got, he'll give nowt.
MOTHER COURAGE: Maybe if we sing. . . .
THE COOK: I've had enough. *Abruptly:* Got a letter from
Utrecht saying mother died of cholera and inn's mine. Here's
the letter if you don't believe me. No business of yours the way
aunty goes on about my mode of existence, but have a look.

MOTHER COURAGE *reads the letter*: Lamb, I'm tired too of always being on the go. I feel like butcher's dog, dragging meat round customers and getting nowt off it. I got nowt left to sell, and folk got nowt left to buy nowt with. Saxony a fellow in rags tried landing me a stack of old books for two eggs, Württemberg they wanted to swap their plough for a titchy bag of salt. What's to plough for? Nowt growing no more, just brambles. In Pomerania villages are s'posed to have started in eating the younger kids, and nuns have been caught sticking folk up.

THE COOK: World's dying out.

MOTHER COURAGE: Sometimes I sees meself driving through hell with me cart selling brimstone, or across heaven with packed lunches for hungry souls. Give me my kids what's left, let's find some place they ain't shooting, and I'd like a few more years undisturbed.

THE COOK: You and me could get that inn going, Courage, think it over. Made up me mind in the night, I did: back to Utrecht with or without you, and starting today.

MOTHER COURAGE: Have to talk to Kattrin. That's a bit quick for me; I'm against making decisions all freezing cold and nowt inside you. Kattrin! *Kattrin climbs out of the cart.* Kattrin, got something to tell you. Cook and I want to go to Utrecht. He's been left an inn there. That'd be a settled place for you, let you meet a few people. Lots of 'em respect somebody mature, looks ain't everything. I'd like it too. I get on with cook. Say one thing for him, got a head for business. We'd have our meals for sure, not bad, eh? And your own bed too; like that, wouldn't you? Road's no life really. God knows how you might finish up. Lousy already, you are. Have to make up our minds, see, we could move with the Swedes, up north, they're somewhere up that way. *She points to the left.* Reckon that's fixed, Kattrin.

THE COOK: Anna, I got something private to say to you.

MOTHER COURAGE: Get back in the cart, Kattrin.

*Kattrin climbs back.*

THE COOK: I had to interrupt, 'cause you don't understand, far as I can see. I didn't think there was need to say it, sticks out a mile. But if it don't, then let me tell you straight, no question of taking her along, not on your life. You get me, eh.

*Kattrin sticks her head out of the cart behind them and listens.*

MOTHER COURAGE: You mean I'm to leave Kattrin back here?

THE COOK: Use your imagination. Inn's got no room. It ain't one of the sort got three bar parlours. Put our backs in it we two'll get a living, but not three, no chance of that. She can keep cart.

MOTHER COURAGE: Thought she might find husband in Utrecht.

THE COOK: Go on, make me laugh. Find a husband, how? Dumb and that scar on top of it. And at her age?

MOTHER COURAGE: Don't talk so loud.

THE COOK: Loud or soft, no getting over facts. And that's another reason why I can't have her in the inn. Customers don't want to be looking at that all the time. Can't blame them.

MOTHER COURAGE: Shut your big mouth. I said not so loud.

THE COOK: Light's on in parson's house. We can try singing.

MOTHER COURAGE: Cooky, how's she to pull the cart on her own? War scares her. She'll never stand it. The dreams she must have. . . . I hear her nights groaning. Mostly after a battle. What's she seeing in those dreams, I'd like to know. She's got a soft heart. Lately I found she'd got another hedgehog tucked away what we'd run over.

THE COOK: Inn's too small. *Calls out:* Ladies and gentlemen, domestic staff and other residents! We are now going to give you a song concerning Solomon, Julius Caesar and other famous personages what had bad luck. So's you can see we're respectable folk, which makes it difficult to carry on, particularly in winter.

*They sing:*

> You saw sagacious Solomon
> You know what came of him.
> To him complexities seemed plain.
> He cursed the hour that gave birth to him

And saw that everything was vain.
How great and wise was Solomon!
The world however didn't wait
But soon observed what followed on.
It's wisdom that had brought him to this state—
How fortunate the man with none!

Yes, the virtues are dangerous stuff in this world, as this fine song proves, better not to have them and have a pleasant life and breakfast instead, hot soup for instance. Look at me: I haven't any but I'd like some. I'm a serving soldier but what good did my courage do me in all them battles, nowt, here I am starving and better have been shit-scared and stayed at home. For why?

You saw courageous Caesar next
You know what he became.
They deified him in his life
Then had him murdered just the same.
And as they raised the fatal knife
How loud he cried: You too, my son!
The world however didn't wait
But soon observed what followed on.
It's courage that had brought him to that state.
How fortunate the man with none!

*Sotto voce:* Don't even look out. *Aloud:* Ladies and gentlemen, domestic staff and other inmates! All right, you may say, gallantry never cooked a man's dinner, what about trying honesty? You can eat all you want then, or anyhow not stay sober. How about it?

You heard of honest Socrates
The man who never lied:
They weren't so grateful as you'd think
Instead the rulers fixed to have him tried
And handed him the poisoned drink.
How honest was the people's noble son!

> The world however didn't wait
> But soon observed what followed on.
> It's honesty that brought him to that state.
> How fortunate the man with none!

Ah yes, they say be unselfish and share what you've got, but how about if you got nowt? It's all very well to say the do-gooders have a hard time, but you still got to have something. Aye, unselfishness is a rare virtue, cause it just don't pay.

> Saint Martin couldn't bear to see
> His fellows in distress.
> He met a poor man in the snow
> And shared his cloak with him, we know.
> Both of them therefore froze to death.
> His place in Heaven was surely won!
> The world however didn't wait
> But soon observed what followed on.
> Unselfishness had brought him to that state.
> How fortunate the man with none!

That's how it is with us. We're respectable folk, stick together, don't steal, don't murder, don't burn places down. And all the time you might say we're sinking lower and lower, and it's true what the song says, and soup is few and far between, and if we weren't like this but thieves and murderers I dare say we'd be eating our fill. For virtues aren't their own reward, only wickednesses are, that's how the world goes and it didn't ought to.

> Here you can see respectable folk
> Keeping to God's own laws.
> So far he hasn't taken heed.
> You who sit safe and warm indoors
> Help to relieve our bitter need!
> How virtuously we had begun!
> The world however didn't wait
> But soon observed what followed on.

> It's fear of God that brought us to that state.
> How fortunate the man with none!

VOICE *from above*: Hey, you there! Come on up! There's hot
soup if you want.

MOTHER COURAGE: Lamb, me stomach won't stand nowt.
'Tain't that it ain't sensible, what you say, but is that your last
word? We got on all right.

THE COOK: Last word. Think it over.

MOTHER COURAGE: I've nowt to think. I'm not leaving her
here.

THE COOK: That's proper senseless, nothing I can do about it
though. I'm not a brute, just the inn's a small one. So now we
better get on up, or there'll be nowt here either and wasted
time singing in the cold.

MOTHER COURAGE: I'll get Kattrin.

THE COOK: Better bring a bit back for her. Scare them if they
sees three of us coming. *Exeunt both.*

*Kattrin climbs out of the cart with a bundle. She looks around
to see if the other two have gone. Then she takes an old pair
of trousers of the cook's and a skirt of her mother's, and lays
them side by side on one of the wheels, so that they are easily
seen. She has finished and is picking up her bundle to go,
when Mother Courage comes back from the house.*

MOTHER COURAGE *with a plate of soup*: Kattrin! Will you
stop there? Kattrin! Where you off to with that bundle? Has
the devil himself taken you over? *She examines the bundle.*
She's packed her things. You been listening? I told him nowt
doing, Utrecht, his rotten inn, what'd we be up to there? You
and me, inn's no place for us. Still plenty to be got out of war.
*She sees the trousers and the skirt.* You're plain stupid. S'pose
I'd seen that, and you gone away? *She holds Kattrin back as
she tries to break away.* Don't you start thinking it's on your
account I given him the push. It was the cart, that's it. Catch
me leaving my cart I'm used to, it ain't you, it's for the cart.
We'll go off in t'other direction, and we'll throw cook's stuff
out so he finds it, silly man. *She climbs in and throws out a
few other articles in the direction of the trousers.* There, he's

out of our business now, and I ain't having nobody else in, ever. You and me'll carry on now. This winter will pass, same as all the others. Get hitched up, it looks like snow.

*They both harness themselves to the cart, then wheel it round and drag it off. When the cook arrives he looks blankly at his kit.*

DURING THE WHOLE OF 1635 MOTHER COURAGE
AND HER DAUGHTER KATTRIN TRAVEL OVER THE
HIGH ROADS OF CENTRAL GERMANY, IN THE WAKE
OF THE INCREASINGLY BEDRAGGLED ARMIES.

*High road.*

*Mother Courage and Kattrin are pulling the cart. They pass a peasant's house inside which there is a voice singing.*

THE VOICE:
> The roses in our arbour
> Delight us with their show:
> They have such lovely flowers
> Repaying all our labour
> After the summer showers.
> Happy are those with gardens now:
> They have such lovely flowers.
>
> When winter winds are freezing
> As through the woods they blow
> Our home is warm and pleasing.
> We fixed the thatch above it
> With straw and moss we wove it.
> Happy are those with shelter now
> When winter winds are freezing.

*Mother Courage and Kattrin pause to listen, then continue pulling.*

JANUARY 1636. THE EMPEROR'S TROOPS ARE
THREATENING THE PROTESTANT TOWN OF HALLE.
THE STONE BEGINS TO SPEAK. MOTHER COURAGE
LOSES HER DAUGHTER AND TRUDGES ON ALONE.
THE WAR IS A LONG WAY FROM BEING OVER.

*The cart is standing, much the worse for wear, alongside a peasant's house with a huge thatched roof, backing on a wall of rock. It is night.*

*An ensign and three soldiers in heavy armour step out of the wood.*

THE ENSIGN: I want no noise now. Anyone shouts, shove your pike into him.

FIRST SOLDIER: Have to knock them up, though, if we're to find a guide.

THE ENSIGN: Knocking sounds natural. Could be a cow bumping the stable wall.

*The soldiers knock on the door of the house. The peasant's wife opens it. They stop her mouth. Two soldiers go in.*

MAN'S VOICE *within*: What is it?

*The soldiers bring out the peasant and his son.*

THE ENSIGN *pointing at the cart, where Kattrin's head has appeared*: There's another one. *A soldier drags her out.* Anyone else live here beside you lot?

THE PEASANTS: This is our son. And she's dumb. Her mother's gone into town to buy stuff. For their business, 'cause so many people's getting out and selling things cheap. They're just passing through. Canteen folk.

THE ENSIGN: I'm warning you, keep quiet, or if there's the least noise you get a pike across your nut. Now I want someone to come with us and show us the path to the town. *Points to the young peasant.* Here, you.

THE YOUNG PEASANT: I don't know no path.

SECOND SOLDIER *grinning*: He don't know no path.

THE YOUNG PEASANT: I ain't helping Catholics.

THE ENSIGN *to the second soldier*: Stick your pike in his ribs.

THE YOUNG PEASANT *forced to his knees, with the pike threatening him*: I won't do it, not to save my life.

FIRST SOLDIER: I know what'll change his mind. *Goes towards the stable.* Two cows and an ox. Listen, you: if you're not reasonable I'll chop up your cattle.

THE YOUNG PEASANT: No, not that!

THE PEASANT'S WIFE *weeps*: Please spare our cattle, captain, it'd be starving us to death.

THE ENSIGN: They're dead if he goes on being obstinate.

FIRST SOLDIER: I'm taking the ox first.

THE YOUNG PEASANT *to his father*: Have I got to? *The wife nods.* Right.

THE PEASANT'S WIFE: And thank you kindly, captain, for sparing us, for ever and ever, Amen.
*The peasant stops his wife from further expressions of gratitude.*

FIRST SOLDIER: I knew the ox was what they minded about most, was I right?
*Guided by the young peasant, the ensign and his men continue on their way.*

THE PEASANT: What are they up to, I'd like to know. Nowt good.

THE PEASANT'S WIFE: Perhaps they're just scouting. What you doing?

THE PEASANT *putting a ladder against the roof and climbing up it*: Seeing if they're on their own. *From the top:* Something moving in the wood. Can see something down by the quarry. And there are men in armour in the clearing. And a gun. That's at least a regiment. God's mercy on the town and everyone in it!

THE PEASANT'S WIFE: Any lights in the town?

THE PEASANT: No. They'll all be asleep. *Climbs down.* If those people get in they'll butcher the lot.

THE PEASANT'S WIFE: Sentries're bound to spot them first.

THE PEASANT: Sentry in the tower up the hill must have been killed, or he'd have blown his bugle.

THE PEASANT'S WIFE: If only there were more of us.

THE PEASANT: Just you and me and that cripple.

THE PEASANT'S WIFE: Nowt we can do, you'd say. . . .

THE PEASANT: Nowt.

THE PEASANT'S WIFE: Can't possibly run down there in the blackness.

THE PEASANT: Whole hillside's crawling with 'em. We could give a signal.

THE PEASANT'S WIFE: What, and have them butcher us too?

THE PEASANT: You're right, nowt we can do.

THE PEASANT'S WIFE *to Kattrin*: Pray, poor creature, pray! Nowt we can do to stop bloodshed. You can't talk, maybe, but at least you can pray. He'll hear you if no one else can. I'll help you. *All kneel, Kattrin behind the two peasants.* Our Father, which art in Heaven, hear Thou our prayer, let not the town be destroyed with all what's in it sound asleep and suspecting nowt. Arouse Thou them that they may get up and go to the walls and see how the enemy approacheth with pikes and guns in the blackness across fields below the slope. *Turning to Kattrin:* Guard Thou our mother and ensure that the watchman sleepeth not but wakes up, or it will be too late. Succour our brother-in-law also, he is inside there with his four children, spare Thou them, they are innocent and know nowt. *To Kattrin, who gives a groan:* One of them's not two yet, the eldest's seven. *Kattrin stands up distractedly.* Our Father, hear us, for only Thou canst help; we look to be doomed, for why, we are weak and have no pike and nowt and can risk nowt and are in Thy hand along with our cattle and all the farm, and same with the town, it too is in Thy hand and the enemy is before the walls in great strength.

*Unobserved, Kattrin has slipped away to the cart and taken from it something which she hides beneath her apron; then she climbs up the ladder on to the stable roof.*

THE PEASANT'S WIFE: Forget not the children, what are in

danger, the littlest ones especially, the old folk what can't move, and every living creature.

THE PEASANT: And forgive us our trespasses as we forgive them that trespass against us. Amen.

*Sitting on the roof, Kattrin begins to beat the drum which she has pulled out from under her apron.*

THE PEASANT'S WIFE: Jesus Christ, what's she doing?

THE PEASANT: She's out of her mind.

THE PEASANT'S WIFE: Quick, get her down.

*The peasant hurries to the ladder, but Kattrin pulls it up on to the roof.*

THE PEASANT'S WIFE: She'll do us in.

THE PEASANT: Stop drumming at once, you cripple!

THE PEASANT'S WIFE: Bringing the Catholics down on us!

THE PEASANT *looking for stones to throw*: I'll stone you.

THE PEASANT'S WIFE: Where's your feelings? Where's your heart? We're done for if they come down on us. Slit our throats, they will. *Kattrin stares into the distance towards the town and carries on drumming.*

THE PEASANT'S WIFE *to her husband*: I told you we shouldn't have allowed those vagabonds on to farm. What do they care if our last cows are taken?

THE ENSIGN *runs in with his soldiers and the young peasant*: I'll cut you to ribbons, all of you!

THE PEASANT'S WIFE: Please, sir, it's not our fault, we couldn't help it. It was her sneaked up there. A foreigner.

THE ENSIGN: Where's the ladder?

THE PEASANT: There.

THE ENSIGN *calls up*: I order you, throw that drum down.

*Kattrin goes on drumming.*

THE ENSIGN: You're all in this together. It'll be the end of you.

THE PEASANT: They been cutting pine trees in that wood. How about if we got one of the trunks and poked her off. . . .

FIRST SOLDIER *to the ensign*: Permission to make a suggestion, sir! *He whispers something in the ensign's ear.* Listen, we got a suggestion could help you. Get down off there and come into town with us right away. Show us which your mother is and we'll see she ain't harmed.

*Kattrin goes on drumming.*

THE ENSIGN *pushes him roughly aside*: She doesn't trust you; with a mug like yours it's not surprising. *Calls up*: Suppose I gave you my word? I can give my word of honour as an officer. *Kattrin drums harder.*

THE ENSIGN: Is nothing sacred to her?

THE YOUNG PEASANT: There's more than her mother involved, sir.

FIRST SOLDIER: This can't go on much longer. They're bound to hear in the town.

THE ENSIGN: We'll have somehow to make a noise that's louder than her drumming. What can we make a noise with?

FIRST SOLDIER: Thought we weren't s'posed to make no noise.

THE ENSIGN: A harmless one, you fool. A peaceful one.

THE PEASANT: I could chop wood with my axe.

THE ENSIGN: Good: you chop. *The peasant fetches his axe and attacks a tree-trunk.* Chop harder! Harder! You're chopping for your life. *Kattrin has been listening, drumming less loudly the while. She now looks wildly round, and goes on drumming.*

THE ENSIGN: Not loud enough. *To the first soldier:* You chop too.

THE PEASANT: Only got the one axe. *Stops chopping.*

THE ENSIGN: We'll have to set the farm on fire. Smoke her out, that's it.

THE PEASANT: It wouldn't help, captain. If the townspeople see a fire here they'll know what's up.

*Kattrin has again been listening as she drums. At this point she laughs.*

THE ENSIGN: Look at her laughing at us. I'm not having that. I'll shoot her down, and damn the consequences. Fetch the harquebus.

*Three soldiers hurry off. Kattrin goes on drumming.*

THE PEASANT'S WIFE: I got it, captain. That's their cart. If we smash it up she'll stop. Cart's all they got.

THE ENSIGN *to the young peasant*: Smash it up. *Calls up:* We're going to smash up your cart if you don't stop drumming. *The young peasant gives the cart a few feeble blows.*

THE PEASANT'S WIFE: Stop it, you animal!
  *Desperately looking towards the cart, Kattrin emits pitiful noises. But she goes on drumming.*
THE ENSIGN: Where are those clodhoppers with the harquebus?
FIRST SOLDIER: Can't have heard nowt in town yet, else we'd be hearing their guns.
THE ENSIGN *calls up*: They can't hear you at all. And now we're going to shoot you down. For the last time: throw down that drum!
THE YOUNG PEASANT *suddenly flings away his plank*: Go on drumming! Or they'll all be killed! Go on, go on. . . .
  *The soldier knocks him down and beats him with his pike. Kattrin starts to cry, but she goes on drumming.*
THE PEASANT'S WIFE: Don't strike his back! For God's sake, you're beating him to death!
  *The soldiers hurry in with the harquebus.*
SECOND SOLDIER: Colonel's frothing at the mouth, sir. We're all for court-martial.
THE ENSIGN: Set it up! Set it up! *Calls up while the gun is being erected*: For the very last time: stop drumming!
  *Kattrin, in tears, drums as loud as she can.* Fire! *The soldiers fire. Kattrin is hit, gives a few more drumbeats and then slowly crumples.*
THE ENSIGN: That's the end of that.
  *But Kattrin's last drumbeats are taken up by the town's cannon.*
  *In the distance can be heard a confused noise of tocsins and gunfire.*
FIRST SOLDIER: She's made it.

# 12

BEFORE FIRST LIGHT. SOUND OF THE FIFES
AND DRUMS OF TROOPS MARCHING OFF
INTO THE DISTANCE.

*In front of the cart Mother Courage is squatting by her daughter. The peasant family are standing near her.*

THE PEASANTS *with hostility*: You must go, missis. There's only one more regiment behind that one. You can't go on your own.
MOTHER COURAGE: I think she's going to sleep. *She sings:*

> Lullaby baby
> What's that in the hay?
> Neighbours' kids grizzle
> But my kids are gay.
> Neighbours' are in tatters
> And you're dressed in lawn
> Cut down from the raiment an
> Angel has worn.
> Neighbours' kids go hungry
> And you shall eat cake
> Suppose it's too crumbly
> You've only to speak.
> Lullaby baby
> What's that in the hay?
> The one lies in Poland
> The other—who can say?

Better if you'd not told her nowt about your brother-in-law's kids.

THE PEASANT: If you'd not gone into town to get your cut it might never of happened.

MOTHER COURAGE: Now she's asleep.

THE PEASANT'S WIFE: She ain't asleep. Can't you see she's passed over?

THE PEASANT: And it's high time you got away yourself. There are wolves around and, what's worse, marauders.

MOTHER COURAGE: Aye.

*She goes and gets a tarpaulin to cover the dead girl with.*

THE PEASANT'S WIFE: Ain't you got nobody else? What you could go to?

MOTHER COURAGE: Aye, one left. Eilif.

THE PEASANT *as Mother Courage covers the dead girl*: Best look for him, then. We'll mind her, see she gets proper burial. Don't you worry about that.

MOTHER COURAGE: Here's money for expenses.

*She counts out coins into the peasant's hands.*

*The peasant and his son shake hands with her and carry Kattrin away.*

THE PEASANT'S WIFE *as she leaves*: I'd hurry.

MOTHER COURAGE *harnessing herself to the cart*: Hope I can pull the cart all right by meself. Be all right, nowt much inside it. Got to get back in business again.

*Another regiment with its fifes and drums marches past in the background.*

MOTHER COURAGE *tugging the cart*: Take me along!

*Singing is heard from offstage:*

> With all its luck and all its danger
> The war is dragging on a bit
> Another hundred years or longer
> The common man won't benefit.
> Filthy his food, no soap to shave him
> The regiment steals half his pay.
> But still a miracle may save him:
> Tomorrow is another day!
>     The new year's come. The watchmen shout.
>     The thaw sets in. The dead remain.
>     Wherever life has not died out
>     It staggers to its feet again.

# NOTES AND VARIANTS

# Texts by Brecht

## NOTE

The effect of the première of *Mother Courage and Her Children*, given in Zürich during the Second World War with the exceptional Therese Giehse in the title part, was to allow the bourgeois press to talk about a Niobe-like tragedy and the heart-rending vitality of all maternal creatures. This despite the pacifist and anti-fascist convictions of the Zürich Schauspielhaus and its predominantly émigré German actors. Thus forewarned, the playwright made certain changes for the Berlin production. What follows is the original text.

### Scene 1, pp. 9–10.

MOTHER COURAGE: . . . Look out for yourselves, you'll need to. And now up we get and on we go.

THE SERGEANT: I don't feel very well.

THE RECRUITER: Perhaps you caught a chill taking your helmet off in that wind.

*The Sergeant snatches back his helmet.*

MOTHER COURAGE: Hey, gimme my papers, you. Someone else might ask to see them, and there'd I be with no papers.

*She puts them all in her pewter box.*

THE RECRUITER *to Eilif*: Have a look at them boots anyway. And then we men'll have one together. And come round behind the cart, I'll show you I got the bounty money on me.

THE SERGEANT: I don't get it, I'm always at the rear. Sergeant's safest job there is. You can send the others up front, cover themselves with glory. Me dinner hour's properly spoiled. Shan't be able to hold nowt down, I know.

MOTHER COURAGE *addressing him*: Mustn't let it prey on you so's you can't eat. Just stay at the rear. Here, take a swig of brandy, man. *Gives him a drink from the cart.*

RECRUITER *has taken Eilif by the arm and is leading him away up stage*: If a bullet's got your name on it there's nowt you can do about it. You drew a cross, that's all. Ten florins bounty money, then you're a gallant fellow fighting for the king and women'll be after you like flies. And you can clobber me free for insulting you. *Exeunt both.*

*Dumb Kattrin, having watched this seduction, makes hoarse noises.*

MOTHER COURAGE: All right, Kattrin, all right. Sergeant's not feeling well, he's superstitious, I hadn't realised. And now let's get moving. Where's Eilif gone?

SWISS CHEESE: Must have gone off with the recruiter. They was talking together the whole time.

## Scene 5, pp. 44–46.

MOTHER COURAGE *to the other*: Can't pay, that it? No money, no schnapps. They give us military marches, but catch them giving men their pay.

SOLDIER: I want my schnapps. I missed the looting. That double-crossing general only allowed an hour's looting in the town. He ain't an inhuman monster, he said. Town must of paid him.

THE CHAPLAIN *stumbles in*: There are people still lying in that yard. The peasant's family. Somebody give me a hand. I need linen.

*The second soldier goes off with him.*

MOTHER COURAGE: I got none. All my bandages was sold to the regiment. I ain't tearing up my officers' shirts for that lot.

CHAPLAIN *calling back*: I need linen, I tell you.

MOTHER COURAGE *rummages in her cart*: I'm giving nowt. They'll never pay, and why, nowt to pay with.

CHAPLAIN *bending over a woman he has carried in*: Why d'you stay around during the gunfire?

PEASANT WOMAN *feebly*: Farm.

MOTHER COURAGE: Catch them abandoning anything. My lovely shirts! Tomorrow officers'll be around and I'll have nowt for 'em. *She throws down one which Kattrin gives to the peasant woman.* What's got into me, giving stuff away? Wasn't me started this war.

FIRST SOLDIER: Those are Protestants. What they have to be Protestants for?

MOTHER COURAGE: They ain't bothering about faith. They lost their farm.

SECOND SOLDIER: They're no Protestants. They're Catholics like us.

FIRST SOLDIER: No way of sorting 'em out in a bombardment.

A PEASANT *brought in by the chaplain*: My arm's gone.

*The painful screams of a child are heard from the house.*

THE CHAPLAIN *to the peasant woman*: Lie where you are.

MOTHER COURAGE: Get that child out of there!

*Kattrin dashes in.*

MOTHER COURAGE *tearing up shirts*: A hundred florins apiece. I'm ruined. Don't shift her as you're doing her bandage, it might be her back. *To Kattrin, who has rescued a baby from the ruins and is cradling it as she walks*: How nice, found another baby to cart around? Give it to its ma this instant, unless you'd have me fighting for hours to get it off you, like last time, d'you hear? *Kattrin pays no attention.* All your victories mean to me is losses. That's enough, padre, come on, easy with my linen for Christ sake.

THE CHAPLAIN: I need more, blood's coming through.

MOTHER COURAGE *referring to Kattrin*: Look at her, happy as a queen in all this misery; give it back at once, its mother's coming round. *As Kattrin reluctantly hands the baby back to its mother, Mother Courage tears up another shirt.* I can't give nowt, catch me, got to think of meself. *To the second soldier*: Don't stand there gawping, you go back and tell them cut out that music, we can see it's a victory with our own eyes. Help yourself to a glass of schnapps, padre, don't argue, I've enough troubles. *She has to climb down off the cart to pull her daughter away from the first soldier, who is drunk.* Thought you'd score another victory, you animal? You're not getting away like that till you've paid. *To the peasant*: Your kid won't go short. *Indicating the woman*: Help yourself to something for her. *To the first soldier*: Then leave that coat, it's stolen any road. *The first soldier goes lurching away. Mother Courage tears up further shirts.*

THE CHAPLAIN: There's still someone under there.

MOTHER COURAGE: Don't worry, I'm tearing up the lot.

## Scene 7, p. 56.

*High road. The chaplain, Mother Courage and Kattrin are pulling the cart. It is filthy and neglected, but hung with new wares none the less.*

MOTHER COURAGE *sings*:

Some people think to live by looting [etc. with one or two small variations not affecting the meaning] . . .

*The refrain 'The new year's come' is played by her on her mouthorgan.*

## Scene 12, p. 61.

THE PEASANTS: You must go, missis. There's only one more regiment behind that one. You can't go on your own.
MOTHER COURAGE: She's still breathing. Maybe she's falling asleep.

The effect of the peasant wars, the greatest disaster in German history, was to draw the teeth of the Reformation. That left business and cynicism. Along with her friends and guests and almost everyone else, Courage—and I say this as an aid to theatrical production—recognises the purely commercial nature of the war; indeed this is what attracts her to it. She believes in the war right to the end. It never even strikes her that in a war you need a big pair of scissors if you are to get your cut. Observers of catastrophes are wrong to imagine that the victims will learn from these. So long as the masses remain the passive *object* of politics they will never be able to view what happens to them as an experiment, merely as a fate; they learn no more from the catastrophe than a guinea pig learns about biology. It is not the playwright's job to open Courage's eyes at the end—she catches a glimpse of something around the middle of the play, at the end of scene 6, then loses sight of it once more—his concern is with the eyes of the audience.

['Anmerkung' from *Versuche* 9, Suhrkamp, Frankfurt 1949, reprinted in *GW Stücke* 4.]

## THE STORY

### Curve of the dramaturgy

*I*

This scene emphasises that things are at the beginning. Courage's canteen business and the new war as new undertakings of a familiar sort. (They begin and they continue; they begin by continuing.) Needed: energy, enterprise, the prospect of new times, arrival of new business, together with new dangers. She longs for war and at the same time fears it. She wants to join in, but as a peaceable business woman, not in a war-like way. She wants to maintain her family during the war and by means of it. She wants to serve the army and also to keep out of its clutches.

Her children: With her eldest son she is afraid of his bravery, but counts on his cleverness. With the second she is afraid of his stupidity but counts on his honesty. With her daughter she is afraid of her pity but counts on her dumbness. Only her fears prove to be justified.

She is anticipating business; she is going to go bankrupt.

The play begins with the entrance (i.e., hanging about) of the men of war. The vast disorder of war begins with order, the vast disorganisation with organisation.

The peaceful landscape and the men of iron. Courage arrives four strong, goes away three strong.

### 2

War as a business idyll. Courage swindles peasants out of a capon; her elder son robs peasants of their oxen. He wins fame and possessions; she profits. She pillages the army somewhat too. The danger for her son becomes more real.

### 3

Being taken prisoner need be no disadvantage to her business. It seems that she had nothing to say against her younger son's joining the army as a paymaster. All she thinks necessary in his case is honesty. This is the finish of him. If he had not been connected with the army he would not have been killed. Her stubborn bargaining over her cart costs her son his life. She stops her daughter from becoming a whore—the only career open to her in wartime, and one which brings good fortune to Yvette. In any case she is no Antigone.

### 4

Courage stifles her human reactions (any kind of outrage, rebellion or criticism) for the sake of her business. She thinks capitulation will do something for her.

### 5

All the same, human reactions sometimes override her business principles. The general's victory leads to financial losses.

### 6

Business, meant to earn her daughter's (peacetime) dowry, leads to her wartime disfigurement. Courage counts on the length of the war, which is helpful to her finances but means spinsterhood for her daughter. Finally for the first time she curses the war which, from a business standpoint, she must needs want.

### 7

Peacetime is pleasant, if also ruinous. Thanks to the peace she does not get her son back, but loses him for good. In her daughter's case peace arrives too late. The son falls because he has applied the principles of war in peacetime. The former camp prostitute Yvette Pottier has prospered as a result of the war and married a colonel. The war starts up again. Will business start up again too?

### 8

Business is on the downgrade. The war is too long. Disorganisation and disorder on every side. In a song Courage (qua beggar) curses all the human virtues as not only uncommercial but positively dangerous. For her daughter's sake she must give up the cook, who could have provided her with a roof over her head. She is bound to the war by pity for her daughter.

### 9

The daughter perishes because of her pity for other people's children. Courage goes on dragging her empty cart, alone, in the wake of the tattered army.

[From Werner Hecht (ed.): *Materialien zu Brechts 'Mutter Courage,'* Frankfurt, Suhrkamp, 1967, pp. 7–9.]

## THREE DIARY NOTES

(i)
Going over *Mother Courage* I am quite pleased to see how war emerges as a vast field akin to the fields of modern physics, in which bodies experience peculiar deviations from their courses. Any calculation about the individual based on peacetime experience proves to be unreliable, bravery is no help, nor is caution, nor honesty, nor crookedness, nor brutality, nor pity: all are equally fatal. We are left with those same forces that turn peace into war, the ones that can't be named.

(ii)
Why is *Courage* a realist work?
It adopts a realist point of view on behalf of the people vis-à-vis all ideologies. To the people war is neither an uprising nor a business operation, merely a disaster.

Its point of view is not a moral one: that is to say, it is ethical, but without being derived from the currently prevailing morality.

The actions of the characters are given motives that can be recognised and allowed for and will facilitate dealing with real people.

The work functions in terms of the present state of consciousness of the majority of mankind.

(iii)

Rehearsing the new production of *Courage* (with Busch, Geschonneck and Lutz). Paying particular attention to the dialectical elements. Cook and Chaplain in scene 8, where peace brings them both to the edge of the precipice, are fighting for their quarters: their respective setbacks make them better people. The two enemies meet amicably on the plane of reminiscent nostalgia for the war.

Working on Ruth's Model book is a grind; but it has to be done if only to show how many things have to be taken into account for a production.

[From Brecht's *Arbeitsjournal*, Suhrkamp 1973, entries for 5 January 1941, 22 April 1941 and 4 June 1951. The new production by the Berliner Ensemble had its première in September 1951 and was then seen at the Paris International Theatre Festival in 1954.]

## THE MOTHER COURAGE MODEL

Now, after the great war, life goes on in our ruined cities, but it is a different life, the life of different or differently composed groups, guided or thwarted by new surroundings, new because so much has been destroyed. The great heaps of rubble are piled on the city's invaluable substructure, the water and drainage pipes, the gas mains and electric cables. Even those large buildings that have remained intact are affected by the damage and rubble around them, and may become an obstacle to planning. Temporary structures must be built and there is always a danger of their becoming permanent. All this is reflected in art, for our way of thinking is part of our way of living. In the theatre we set up models to fill the gap. They immediately meet with strong opposition from all supporters of the old ways, of the routine that masquerades as experience and of the conventionality that calls itself creative freedom. And they are endangered by those who take them up without having learned to use them. While meant to simplify matters, they are not simple to handle. They were designed not to make thought unnecessary, but to provoke it; not to replace but to compel artistic creation.

First of all we must imagine that the information which the printed text provides about certain events—in this case the adventures of Mother Courage and the losses she incurs—has to some extent been complemented; it has now been established that when the woman's dead son was brought to her she was sitting beside her mute daughter, and so on—the kind of information which an artist painting some historic incident can arrive at by questioning eye-witnesses. Later he can still change certain details as for one reason or another he may think advisable. Until one has learned to copy (and construct) models in a living and intelligent way, one had better not copy too much. Such things as the cook's makeup or Mother Courage's costume should not be imitated. The model should not be used to excess.

Pictures and descriptions of a performance are not enough. One does not learn much by reading that a character moves in a particular direction after a given sentence, even if the tone of the sentence, the way of walking, and a convincing motive can be supplied—which is very difficult. The persons available for the imitation are not the same as those of the pattern; with them it would not have come into being. Anyone who deserves the name of artist is unique; he represents something universal, but in his own individual way. He can neither be perfectly imitated nor give a perfect imitation. Nor is it so important for artists to imitate art as to imitate life. The use of models is a particular kind of art, and there is a limit to what can be learned from it. The aim must be neither to copy the pattern exactly nor to break away from it too quickly.

In studying what follows—a number of explanations and discoveries emerging from the rehearsal of a play—one should above all be led by the solutions of certain problems to consider the problems themselves.

## Music

Paul Dessau's music for *Mother Courage* is not meant to be particularly easy; like the stage set, it left something to be supplied by the audience; in the act of listening they had to link the voices with the melody. Art is not a land of Cockaigne. In order to make the transition to the musical items, to let the music have its say, we lowered a musical emblem from the grid whenever there was a song which did not spring directly from the action, or which did spring from it but remained clearly apart. This consisted of a trumpet, a drum, a flag, and electric globes that lit up; a slight and delicate thing, pleasant to look at, even if scene 9 found it badly damaged. Some people regarded this as sheer playfulness, as an unrealistic element. But on the one hand playfulness in the theatre should not be condemned out of hand as long as it is kept within bounds, and on the other it was not wholly unrealistic, for it served to set the music apart from the reality of the action. We made use of it as a visible sign of the shift to another artistic level—that of music—and in order to give the right impression that these were musical insertions, rather than to lead people to think quite mistakenly that the songs 'sprang from the action'. People who object to this are quite simply opposed to anything intermittent, inorganic, pieced-together—this chiefly because they object to any shattering of illusion. What they ought to have objected to was not the tangible symbol of music, but the manner of fitting the musical numbers into the play: i.e., as insertions.

The musicians were placed so that they could be seen, in a box beside the stage—thus their performances became little concerts, independent contributions made at suitable points in the play. The box communicated with the stage, so that a musician or two could occasionally go backstage for trumpet calls or when music occurred as part of the action.

We began with the overture. It was a bit thin, for it was performed by only four musicians; still, it was a reasonably ceremonious preparation for the confusions of war.

## Stage design

For the production we are describing, at the Deutsches Theater in Berlin, we used the well-known model devised by Teo Otto during the war for the Zürich Schauspielhaus. There was a permanent framework of huge screens, making use of such materials as one would expect to find in the military encampments of the seventeenth century: tenting, wooden posts lashed together with ropes, etc. Three-dimensional structures, realistic both as to construction and as to material, were placed on the stage to represent such buildings as the parsonage and the peasants' house, but in artistic abbreviation, only so much being shown as was necessary for the action. Coloured projections were thrown on the cyclorama, and the revolving stage was used to give the impression of travel—we varied the size and position of the screens and used them only for the camp scenes, so as to distinguish these from the scenes on the highway. The Berlin stage designer made his own versions of the buildings (in scenes 2, 4, 5, 9, 10 and 11), but on the same principle. We dispensed with the background projections used in Zürich and hung the names of the various countries over the stage in large black letters. We used an even, white light, as much of it as our equipment permitted. In this way we eliminated any vestige of 'atmosphere' that could easily have given the incidents a romantic tinge. We retained almost everything else down to the smallest details (chopping block, hearth, etc.), particularly the admirable positionings of the cart. This last was very important because it determined much of the grouping and movement from the outset.

Surprisingly little is lost by the sacrifice of complete freedom of 'artistic creation'. You have to start somewhere, with something, and it may as well be with something that has already been fully thought out. Freedom will be acquired through the principle of contradiction, which is continually active and vocal in all of us.

## Realistic theatre and illusion

Writing in 1826, Goethe spoke of the 'inadequacy of the English wooden stage' of Shakespeare's day. He says: 'There is no trace here of the aids to naturalness to which we have gradually become accustomed through the improvement in machinery, in the art of perspective and in costuming.' 'Who,' he asks, 'would tolerate such a thing today? Under those conditions Shakespeare's plays would become highly interesting fairy tales, narrated by a number of persons who tried to increase their effectiveness somewhat by making up as the characters, by coming and going and carrying out the movements necessary to the story, but left it to the audience to imagine as many paradises and palaces as they pleased on the empty stage.'

Since he wrote these words, the mechanical equipment of our theatres has been improving for a hundred years, and 'aids to naturalness' have led to such emphasis on illusion that we late-comers would be more inclined to put up with Shakespeare on an empty stage than with a Shakespeare who had ceased to require or provoke any use of the imagination.

In Goethe's day such improvement as had been made in the mechanics of illusion was relatively harmless, since the machinery was so imperfect, so much 'in the childhood of its beginnings', that theatre itself was still a reality and both imagination and ingenuity could still be employed to turn nature into art. The sets were still theatrical displays, in which the stage designer gave an artistic and poetic interpretation of the places concerned.

The bourgeois classical theatre occupied a happy halfway point on the road to naturalistic illusionism. Stage machinery provided enough elements of illusion to improve the representation of some aspects of reality, but not so much as to make the audience feel that they were no longer in a theatre; art had not yet come to signify the obliteration of all indications that art is at work. Since there was no electricity, lighting effects were still primitive; where poor taste decreed sunset effects, poor equipment prevented total enchantment. The Meiningers' authentic costumes came later; they were usually magnificent, though not always beautiful, and they were after all compensated by an inauthentic manner of speaking. In short, theatre remained the theatre, at least where it failed in its business of deception. Today the restoration of the theatre's reality as theatre is a precondition for any realistic representation of human relations. Too much heightening of the illusion in the setting, along with a 'magnetic' manner of acting which gives the spectator the illusion of being present at a fleeting, fortuitous 'real' event, create such an impression of naturalness that one can no longer interpose one's judgment, imagination or reactions, and must simply conform by sharing in the experience and becoming one of 'nature's' objects. The illusion created by the theatre must be a partial one, so that it can always be recognised as illusion. Reality, however completely represented, must be changed by art, in order that it may be seen to be subject to change and treated as such.

That is why we are demanding naturalness today—because we want to change the nature of our human relations.

## Elements of illusion

No doubt the sight of the cyclorama behind a completely empty stage (in the prologue and in the seventh and last scenes) creates the illusion of a flat landscape with the sky above it. There is no objection to this, because there must be some stirring of poetry in the soul of the spectator if such an illusion is to come about. Thanks to the ease with which it is created, the actors are able to suggest by their manner of playing, at the beginning, that a wide horizon lies open to the business enterprise of the little family of provisioners, then at the end that the exhausted seeker after fortune is faced by boundless devastation. And we can always hope that this substantive impression of the play will combine with a formal one: that when the spectator sees the empty stage, soon to be inhabited, he will be able to share in the initial void from which everything arises. On this tabula rasa, he knows, the actors have been working for weeks, testing first one detail, then another, coming to know the incidents of the chronicle by portraying them, and portraying them by judging them. And now the play is starting and Mother Courage's cart comes rolling on to the stage.

If in big matters such a thing as a beautiful approximation is possible, in matters of detail it is not. A realistic portrayal requires carefully worked-out detail in costumes and props, for here the imagination of the audience can add nothing. All implements connected with working and eating must have been most lovingly made. And the costumes, of course, cannot be as for a folklore festival; they must show signs of individuality and social class. They have been worn for a longer or shorter time, are made of cheaper or more expensive material, are well or not so well taken care of, etc.

The costumes for this production of *Mother Courage* were by [Kurt] Palm.

## What is a performance of *Mother Courage* and Her Children primarily meant to show?

That in wartime the big profits are not made by little people. That war, which is a continuation of business by other means, makes the human virtues fatal even to their possessors. That no sacrifice is too great for the struggle against war.

## Prologue

By way of a prologue, Mother Courage and her little family were shown on their way to the war zone. Mother Courage sang her business song from scene 1 (so that in scene 1 her answer 'In business' is followed immediately by the sergeant's question: 'Halt! Who are you lot with?'). After the overture, to spare the performer the exertion of singing against the rumbling of the revolve, the first stanza was played on a record, the house being darkened. Then the prologue begins.

## The long road to war

The linen half-curtain, on which in the following the titles of the scenes are projected, opens and Mother Courage's cart is rolled forward against the movement of the revolve.

The cart is a cross between a military vehicle and a general store. A sign affixed to the side of it says: 'Second Finnish Regiment' and another 'Mother Courage, Groceries'. On the canvas Swedish pork sausages are displayed next to a flag with a price tag indicating 'Four Florins'. The cart will undergo several changes in the course of the chronicle. There will be sometimes more, sometimes less merchandise hanging on it, the canvas will be dirtier or cleaner, the letters on the signs will be faded and then again freshly painted, depending on the state of business. Now, at the start, it is clean and richly covered with wares.

The cart is pulled by the two sons. They sing the second stanza of Mother Courage's Business Song: 'Generals, how can you make them face it— / March off to death without a brew?' On the box sit dumb Kattrin, playing the Jew's harp, and Mother Courage. Courage is sitting in lazy comfort, swaying with the cart and yawning. Everything, including her one backward glance, indicates that the cart has come a long way.

We had conceived of the song as a dramatic entrance, lusty and cocky—we had the last scene of the play in mind. But Weigel saw it as a realistic business song and suggested that it be used to picture the long journey to the war. Such are the ideas of great actors.

Once this was settled, it seemed to us that by showing the business woman's long journey to the war zone we would be showing clearly enough that she was an active and voluntary participant in the war. But certain reviews and many discussions with persons who had seen the play showed that a good many people regarded Mother Courage merely as a representative of the 'little people' who 'become involved in the war in spite of themselves', who are 'helpless victims of the war', and so on. A deeply engrained habit leads the theatregoer to pick out the more emotional utterances of the characters and overlook everything else. Like descriptions of landscapes in novels, references to business are received with boredom. The 'business atmosphere' is simply the air one breathes and as such requires no special mention. And so, regardless of all our efforts to represent the war as an aggregate of business deals, the discussions showed time and time again that people regarded it as a timeless abstraction.

## Too short can be too long

The two stanzas of the opening song plus the pause between them during which the cart rolls silently along, take up a certain amount of time, too much time it seemed to us at first in rehearsal. But when we

cut the second stanza, the prologue seemed longer, and when we prolonged the pause between the stanzas, it seemed shorter.
[ . . . ]


I


### THE BUSINESS WOMAN ANNA FIERLING,
### KNOWN AS MOTHER COURAGE, ENCOUNTERS
### THE SWEDISH ARMY.

*Recruiters are going about the country looking for cannon fodder.
Mother Courage introduces her mixed family, acquired in various
theatres of war, to a sergeant. The canteen woman defends her sons
against the recruiters with a knife. She sees that her sons are listening to the recruiters and predicts that the sergeant will meet an early
death. To make her children afraid of the war, she has them draw
black crosses as well. Thanks to a small business deal, she nevertheless loses her brave son. And the sergeant leaves her with a
prophecy:*

'Want the war to nourish you?
You must feed it something too.'


## Overall arrangement

*Recruiters are going about the country looking for cannon fodder.* On
the empty stage the sergeant and the recruiter are standing right front
on the lookout, complaining in muffled voices of the difficulty of finding cannon fodder for their general. The city of which the sergeant
speaks is assumed to be in the orchestra. Mother Courage's cart appears and the recruiters' mouths water at the sight of the young men.
The sergeant cries 'Halt!' and the cart stops.

*Mother Courage introduces her mixed family, acquired in various
theatres of war, to a sergeant.* The professionals of commerce and of
war meet, the war can start. At the sight of the military, the Fierlings
may hesitate for a moment as though afraid: the soldiers on their own
side are also enemies; the army gives, but it also takes. Mother
Courage's 'Morning, sergeant' is spoken in the same curt, military
monotone as his 'Morning, all.' Climbing down from her cart, she
makes it clear that she regards showing her papers as a formality, su-
perfluous among professionals ('All right, we'll run through the

whole routine'). She introduces her little family, acquired in various theatres of war, in a jocular tone: she puts on a bit of a 'Mother Courage' act.

The cart and the children are on the left, the recruiters on the right. Mother Courage crosses over with her tin box full of papers. She has been summoned, but she is also sallying forth to scout and do business. She describes her children from the other side of the stage, as though better able to take them in from a distance. The recruiter makes forays behind her back, stalking the sons, tempting them. The pivotal point is in the lines: 'I bet you could do with a good pistol, or a belt buckle?' and 'I could do with something else.'

*The canteen woman defends her sons against the recruiters with a knife.* The sergeant leaves her standing there and goes over to the sons, followed by the recruiter. He thumps their chests, feels their calves. He goes back and stands before Mother Courage: 'Why aren't they in the army?' The recruiter has stayed with the sons: 'Let's see if you're a chicken.' Mother Courage runs over, thrusts herself between the recruiter and her son: 'He's a chicken.' The recruiter goes over to the sergeant (on the right) and complains: 'He was crudely offensive'; Mother Courage snatches her Eilif away. The sergeant tries to reason, but Mother Courage pulls a knife and stands there in a rage, guarding her sons.

*Mother Courage sees that her sons are listening to the recruiter and predicts that the sergeant will meet an early death.* Again she goes over to the sergeant ('Give me your helmet'). Her children follow her and look on, gaping. The recruiter makes a flank movement, comes up to Eilif from behind and speaks to him.

When after some hesitation the sergeant has drawn his black cross, the children, satisfied, go back to the cart, but the recruiter follows them. And when Mother Courage turns ('I've got to take advantage'), she sees the recruiter between her sons; he has his arms around their shoulders.

*To make her children afraid of the war, Mother Courage has them draw black crosses as well.* The rebellion in her own ranks is in full swing. She runs angrily behind her cart to paint black crosses for her children. When she returns to the cart's shaft with the helmet, the recruiter, grinning, leaves the children to her and goes back (right) to the sergeant. When the sombre ceremony is over, Mother Courage goes to the sergeant, returns his helmet, and with fluttering skirts climbs up on the seat of the cart. The sons have harnessed themselves, the cart starts moving. Mother Courage has mastered the situation.

*Because of a small business deal, she nevertheless loses her brave
son.* But the sergeant has only been half defeated; on the recruiter's advice, he offers to make a purchase. Electrified, Mother Courage climbs
down from the cart and the sergeant draws her off left behind the cart.
While the deal is in progress, the recruiter takes the harness off Eilif
and leads him away. Kattrin sees this, climbs down from the cart and
tries in vain to call her mother's attention to Eilif's disappearance. But
Mother Courage is deep in her bargaining. Only after she has snapped
her moneybag shut does she notice his absence. For a moment she has
to sit down on the cart shaft, still holding her buckles. Then she angrily flings them into the cart, and the family, with one less member,
moves gloomily off.

*And the sergeant leaves her with a prophecy.* Laughing, he predicts
that if she wants to live off the war, she will also have to give the war
its due.

[ ... ]

## The recruiters

The empty stage of the prologue was transformed into a specific lo-
cality by means of a few clumps of wintry grass marking the edge
of a highway. Here the military men stand waiting, freezing in their
armour.

The great disorder of war begins with order, disorganisation with
organisation. The troublemakers have troubles of their own. We hear
complaints to the effect that it takes intelligence to get a war started.
The military are businessmen. The sergeant has a little book that he
consults, the recruiter has a map to help him fight with geography.
The fusion of war and business cannot be established too soon.

## Grouping

There will be some difficulty in persuading the actors playing the sergeant and the recruiter to stay together and in one place until Mother
Courage's cart appears. In our theatre, groups always show a strong
tendency to break up, partly because each actor believes he can
heighten audience interest by moving about and changing his position, and partly because he wants to be alone, so as to divert the
attention of the audience from the group to himself. But there is no
reason not to leave the military men together; on the contrary, both
the image and the argument would be impaired by a change of
position.

## Changes of position

Positions should be retained as long as there is no compelling reason
for changing them—and a desire for variety is not a compelling reason. If one gives in to a desire for variety, the consequence is a deval-
uation of all movement on the stage; the spectator ceases to look for
a specific meaning behind each movement, he stops taking movement
seriously. But, especially at the crucial points in the action, the full
impact of a change of position must not be weakened. Legitimate variety is obtained by ascertaining the crucial points and planning the
arrangement around them. For example, the recruiters have been listening to Mother Courage; she has succeeded in diverting and enter-
taining them with her talk and so putting them in a good humour; so
far there has been only one ominous circumstance: the sergeant has
asked for her papers; but he has not examined them—his only purpose was to prolong their stay. She takes the next step (physically too;
she goes up to the sergeant, takes hold of his belt buckle, and says: 'I
bet you could do with a belt-buckle?'), she tries to sell them something, and that is when the recruiters spring into action. The sergeant
says ominously: 'I could do with something else' and along with the
recruiter goes over to the sons at the cart's shaft. The recruiters look
the sons over as they would horses. The crucial point is accented
when the sergeant goes back to Mother Courage, comes to a standstill
before her, and asks: 'Why are they dodging their military service?'
(The effect of such movements should not be weakened by having the
actors speak during them.) If changes of position are needed to make
certain developments clear to the audience, the movement must be
utilised to express something significant for the action and for this
particular moment; if nothing of the sort can be found, it is advisable
to review the whole arrangement up to this point; it will probably be
seen to be at fault, because the sole purpose of an arrangement is to
express the action, and the action (it is to be hoped) involves a logical
development of incidents, which the arrangement need only present.

## On details

On the brightly lighted stage every detail, even the smallest, must of
course be acted out to the full. This is especially true of actions
which on our stage are glossed over almost as a matter of principle,
such as payment on conclusion of a sale. Here Weigel devised (for
the sale of the buckle in 1, the sale of the capon in 2, the sale of
drinks in 5 and 6, the handing out of the burial money in 12, etc.) a

little gesture of her own: she audibly snaps shut the leather money-bag that she wears slung from her neck. It is indeed difficult in rehearsals to resist the impatience of actors who are in the habit of trying to sweep an audience off its feet, and to work out the details painstakingly and inventively in accordance with the principle of epic theatre: *one thing after another*. Even minute details are very revealing, e.g., the fact that when the recruiters step up to her sons and feel their muscles as if they were horses, Mother Courage displays maternal pride for a moment, until the sergeant's question ('Why are they dodging their military service?') shows her the danger their qualities put them in: then she rushes between her sons and the recruiters. The pace at rehearsals should be slow, if only to make it possible to work out details; determining the pace of the performance is another matter and comes later.

## A detail

In pulling a knife, Mother Courage shows no savagery. She is merely showing how far she will go in defending her children. The performer must show that Mother Courage is familiar with such situations and knows how to handle them.

*Mother Courage has her children draw lots.* Only by a mild tirade and by eloquently averting her face when Swiss Cheese draws his slip from the helmet—in other words by a slightly exaggerated display of impartiality (see for yourself, no sleight-of-hand, no tricks) does the actress show that Mother Courage knows she has been tampering with fate—otherwise she fully believes what she says, namely, that in certain situations certain of her children's qualities and defects could be fatal.

*Mother Courage predicts that the sergeant will meet an early death.* We discovered that Mother Courage had to turn around towards Eilif before stepping up to the sergeant to let him draw his lot. Otherwise it would not have been understood that she does this in order to frighten her warlike son away from the war.

*The belt-buckle deal.* Mother Courage loses her son to the recruiter because she can't resist the temptation to sell a belt buckle. After climbing down from the cart to bring the sergeant the buckle, she must at first show a certain amount of distrust by looking around anxiously for the recruiter. Once the sergeant, seizing the string of buckles, has drawn her behind the cart, her distrust shifts to the area of business. When she goes to get schnapps for the sergeant, she takes the buckle, which has not yet been paid for, out of his hands; and she bites into the coin. The sergeant is dismayed at her distrust.

If the distrust at the beginning were omitted, we should have a stupid, utterly uninteresting woman, or a person with a passion for business but no experience. The distrust must not be absent, it must merely be too weak to do any good.

## Pantomime

The recruiter must act out the scene where he removes the harness from Eilif ('women'll be after you like flies'). He is freeing him from his yoke.

He has forced a florin on him; holding out his fist with the florin in it in front of him, Eilif goes off as if in a trance.

## Proportion

Weigel showed a masterful sense of proportion in playing Mother Courage's reaction to the abduction of her brave son. She showed dismay rather than horror. In becoming a soldier, her son has not been lost, he is merely in danger. And she will lose other children. To show that she knows very well why Eilif is no longer with her, Weigel let her string of belt buckles drag on the ground and threw it angrily into the cart after holding it between her legs while sitting on the shaft for a few moments to rest. And she does not look her daughter in the face as she puts her into Eilif's harness.

2

### BEFORE THE FORTRESS OF WALLHOF MOTHER COURAGE MEETS HER BRAVE SON AGAIN.

*Mother Courage sells provisions at exorbitant prices in the Swedish camp; while driving a hard bargain over a capon, she makes the acquaintance of an army cook who is to play an important part in her life. The Swedish general brings a young soldier into his tent and honours him for his bravery. Mother Courage recognises her lost son in the young soldier; taking advantage of the meal in Eilif's honour, she gets a steep price for her capon. Eilif relates his heroic deed and Mother Courage, while plucking her capon in the kitchen adjoining the tent, expresses opinions about rotten generals. Eilif does a sword dance and his mother answers with a song. Eilif hugs his mother and gets a slap in the face for putting himself in danger with his heroism.*

## Overall arrangement

*Mother Courage sells provisions at exorbitant prices in the Swedish camp before the fortress of Wallhof; while driving a hard bargain over a capon she makes the acquaintance of an army cook who is to play an important part in her life.* In this scene the movement occurs at the pivotal point ('You know what I'm going to do?'). The cook stops peeling his carrots, fishes a piece of rotten meat out of the garbage barrel and takes it over to the butcher's block. Courage's attempt at blackmail has failed.

*The Swedish general brings a young soldier into his tent and makes a short speech commending him for his bravery.* A drumroll outside the tent announces the arrival of highly placed persons. It need not be clear whether the general drinks in order to honour the soldier or honours the soldier in order to drink. Meanwhile in the kitchen adjoining the tent the cook is preparing the meal. Courage stays right there with her capon.

*Mother Courage recognises her lost son in the young soldier; taking advantage of the meal in Eilif's honour, she gets a steep price for her capon.* Mother Courage is overcome with joy at seeing her son, but not too overcome to turn Eilif's reappearance to her business advantage. Meanwhile, the general gets the chaplain to bring him a spill to light his clay pipe.

*Eilif relates his heroic deed and Mother Courage, while plucking her capon in the kitchen, expresses opinions about rotten generals.* At first the mother beams as she listens to the story, then her face clouds over, and in the end she throws her capon angrily into the tub in front of her. Resuming her work, she lets it be known what she thinks of the general; at the same time the general in the tent shows her son on the map what new deeds of heroism he needs him for.

*Eilif does a sword dance and his mother answers with a song.* Eilif does his sword dance front stage near the partition between tent and kitchen. Mother Courage creeps up to the partition to finish the song. Then she goes back to her tub but remains standing.

*Eilif hugs his mother and gets a slap in the face for putting himself in danger with his heroism.*

## The capon deal

The bargaining over the capon between Courage and the cook served among other things to establish the beginning of their tender relationship. Both showed pleasure in the bargaining, and the cook expressed his admiration not only for her ready tongue but also for the shrewdness with which she exploited the honouring of her son for business purposes. Courage in turn was amused at the way the cook fished the chunk of rotten beef out of the garbage barrel with the tip of his long meat knife and carried it, carefully as though it were a precious object—though to be kept at a safe distance from one's nose—over to his kitchen table. The actor Bildt played the scene brilliantly, making the cook, a Don Juan fired by budding passion, prepare the capon with theatrical elegance. This dumb show, it should be observed, was performed with restraint, so that it did not distract from the scene in the tent.

Bildt even took the trouble to acquire a Dutch accent with the help of a Dutchman.

[ . . . ]

## The general

The general was made into something of a cliché. Too much gruff bluster, and the performance showed too little about the ruling class. It would have been better to make him an effete Swedish aristocrat, who honours the brave soldier as a matter of routine action, almost absently. If this had been done, his very entrance—he is drunk, supports himself on the guest of honour, and heads straight for the wine jug—would have been more instructive. As it was, one saw little more than rowdy drunkenness.

[ . . . ]

## The war of religion

The general's treatment of the chaplain is meant to show the role of religion in a war of religion. This was played rather crudely. The general has him bring the burning spill for his pipe and contemptuously pours wine over his coat; with his eyes on Eilif, the chaplain wipes the hem of his cassock, half protesting, half taking it as a joke. He is not invited to sit down to table like the young murderer, nor is he given anything to drink. But what shows his position most clearly is the undignified way, resulting from the indignity of his position, with which he sits down at table and pours himself wine when the general leads the young soldier, in whose presence all this is enacted, to the map on the tent wall, thereby leaving the table unoccupied. This position is the source of the chaplain's cynicism.

## Eilif's dance

The brave son's short sword dance must be executed with passion as well as ease. The young man is imitating a dance he has seen somewhere. It is not easy to make such things evident.

Costume: Eilif has a cheap, dented breastplate and is still wearing his frayed trousers. Not until scene 8 (the outbreak of peace) does he wear expensive clothing and gear; he dies rich.

## A detail

During her angry speech about rotten generals Courage plucks her capon violently, giving the plucking a kind of symbolic significance. Brief bursts of laughter from the amused cook interrupt her blasphemies.

[ . . . ]

## 3

### MOTHER COURAGE SWITCHES FROM THE LUTHERAN TO THE CATHOLIC CAMP AND LOSES HER HONEST SON SWISS CHEESE.

*Black-marketing in ammunition. Mother Courage serves a camp whore and warns her daughter not to take up with soldiers. While Courage flirts with the cook and the chaplain, dumb Kattrin tries on the whore's hat and shoes. Surprise attack. First meal in the Catholic camp. Conversation between brother and sister and arrest of Swiss Cheese. Mother Courage mortgages her cart to the camp whore in order to ransom Swiss Cheese. Courage haggles over the amount of the bribe. She haggles too long and hears the volley that lays Swiss Cheese low. Dumb Kattrin stands beside her mother to wait for the dead Swiss Cheese. For fear of giving herself away, Courage denies her dead son.*

### Overall arrangement

During the whole scene the cart stands left with its shaft pointed towards the audience, so that those to the left of it are not seen by those on the right. Centre rear there is a flagpole, right front a barrel serving as a dining table. The scene is divided into four parts: *The surprise at-*

*tack, The arrest of the honest son, The bargaining, The denial.* After the first two parts the half-curtain is drawn; after the third part the stage is darkened.

*Black-marketing in ammunition.* Mother Courage enters from the left, followed by an ordnance officer who is trying to talk her into something. For a moment she stands front stage with him; after 'Not at that price', she turns away from him and sits down on a box near the cart, where Swiss Cheese is already sitting. The business is conducted in an undertone. Kattrin is called away from taking down the washing and goes behind the cart left with the ordnance officer. Courage has started mending Swiss Cheese's pants; while working, she admonishes him to be honest. Returning from the other side of the cart, the ordnance officer takes him away with him. This and the following scenes have the tone of an idyll.

*Mother Courage serves a camp whore and warns her daughter not to take up with soldiers.* Taking her sewing, Courage sits down with the Pottier woman. Kattrin listens to their conversation as she takes the washing off the line. After her song, Pottier, with a conspicuously whorish gait, goes behind the cart.

*While Courage flirts with the cook and the chaplain, dumb Kattrin tries on the whore's hat and shoes.* After some brief banter, Mother Courage leads her guests behind the cart for a glass of wine and they strike up a political conversation. After the inserted sentence 'This is a war of faith', the cook ironically starts singing the hymn 'A stronghold sure'. This gives Kattrin time to try on Yvette's hat and shoes.

*Surprise attack.* The fixed point amid all the running and shouting of the surprise attack is the chaplain, who stands still and gets in everybody's way. The rest of the arrangement follows from the printed text.

*First meal in the Catholic camp.* The chaplain, now Mother Courage's potboy, joins the little family around the cooking pot; Swiss Cheese keeps slightly to one side; he wants to get away.

*Conversation between brother and sister and arrest of Swiss Cheese.* The conversation between brother and sister takes place at the improvised dining table. When Kattrin sees the spy behind the cart, she tries to stop her brother from climbing into it. When Courage comes back with the chaplain, Kattrin runs towards her as far as the centre of the stage. Courage, the chaplain and Kattrin group themselves around the table, waiting for the Catholics.

*Mother Courage tries to mortgage her wagon to the camp whore in order to ransom Swiss Cheese.* The chaplain runs to meet Courage;

she is exhausted and he catches her in his arms in front of the cart. She quickly frees herself from his embrace, which has restored her strength a little, and starts thinking. Her plan is all ready when Pottier comes along with the colonel. Pottier leaves the colonel standing there, runs over to Courage, gives her the kiss of Judas, runs back to her cavalier, and then crawls avidly into the cart. Courage pulls her out, curses her, and sends her off with a push to negotiate over Swiss Cheese.

*Mother Courage haggles over the amount of the bribe.* Courage has set Kattrin and the chaplain to washing glasses and scouring knives, so creating a certain atmosphere of siege. Standing centre stage between her family and the whore, she refuses to give up her cart entirely—she has fought too hard for it. She sits down again to scour knives and does not stand up when Pottier comes back with the news that the soldiers are asking two hundred florins. Now she is willing to pay.

*Mother Courage hears the volley that lays Swiss Cheese low.* No sooner has Courage sent Pottier away than she suddenly stands up and says: 'I think I bargained too long.' The volley rings out, the chaplain leaves her and goes behind the wagon. It grows dark.

*For fear of giving herself away, Courage denies her dead son.* Yvette walks slowly out from behind the wagon. She scolds Courage, warns her not to give herself away, and brings Kattrin out from behind the wagon. Her face averted, Kattrin goes to her mother and stands behind her. Swiss Cheese is brought in. His mother goes over to him and denies him.

## Movements and groupings

The arrangement of the movements and groupings must follow the rhythm of the story and give pictorial expression to the action.

In scene 3 a camp idyll is disrupted by the enemy's surprise attack. The idyll should be composed from the start in such a way as to make it possible to show a maximum of disruption. It must leave room for people to run to and fro in clearly laid-out confusion; the parts of the stage must be able to change their functions.

At the beginning of the scene Kattrin is hanging out washing on a clothes-line stretched between the cart and the cannon right rear so that Courage can hurriedly take it down at the end of the scene. In order to rescue her washing, Courage must go diagonally right across the stage. Kattrin sits huddled by the barrel right front, where at the beginning Yvette was being served as a customer; Courage takes soot from the cart and brings it to the barrel to rub on her daughter's face. The same place which up until then had been devoted exclusively to business is now the scene of a private incident. Carrying the cash-box, Swiss Cheese enters diagonally from right rear to the cart left front in such a way that his path crosses that of Courage hurrying to her daughter. First she runs a few steps past him, but she has seen the cash box and turns round towards him just as he is about to enter the cart. She stands for a moment like a hen between two endangered chicks, undecided which to save first. While she is smearing her daughter's face, her son hides the cash box in the cart; she cannot reprove him until she has finished with her daughter and he comes back out of the cart. She is still standing beside him when the chaplain rushes out from behind the cart and points to the Swedish flag. Courage runs to it centre rear and takes it down.

The camp idyll that is disrupted by the attack must be divided into distinct parts. After the shady little deal in black-market ammunition has been completed by the cart steps, Swiss Cheese followed by the ordnance officer goes out right. The ordnance officer recognises the camp whore who is sitting by the barrel, sewing her hat; he looks away in disgust. Yvette shouts something after him, and then, when the centre of gravity has shifted to the right side of the stage, Courage also comes slowly over to the barrel. (A little later Kattrin follows, coming out from behind the cart and starting once more to hang up the washing.) The two women talk and Kattrin listens as she hangs up the washing. Yvette sings her song. With a provocative gait, she goes out from right front to left rear. Kattrin watches her and is admonished by her mother. The cook and the chaplain come in from the right rear. After a brief bit of banter during which they attract the attention of the audience to Kattrin by the attention they pay to her, Mother Courage leads them behind the wagon. The political discussion and Kattrin's pantomine follow. She imitates Yvette, walking over the same ground. The alarm begins with the ordnance officer and soldiers running in from right rear. The cook goes out in that direction after Courage has run to the cannon to rescue her washing and Kattrin to the barrel to hide her feet.

## Important

Courage's unflagging readiness to work is important. She is hardly ever seen not working. It is her energy and competence that make her lack of success so shattering.

## A tiny scene

The tiny scene at the beginning of 3, in which army property is black-marketed, shows the general and matter-of-fact corruption in army camps during the great war of religion. The honest son listens with half an ear, as to something quite usual, his mother does not conceal the crooked business from him, but admonishes him to be honest because he is not bright. His heeding of this advice is going to cost him his life.

## Yvette Pottier

Kattrin has the example of Yvette before her. She herself must work hard; the whore drinks and lolls about. For Kattrin too the only form of love available in the midst of the war would be prostitution. Yvette sings a song showing that other forms of love lead to grave trouble. At times the whore becomes powerful by selling herself at a high price. Mother Courage, who only sells boots, must struggle desperately to defend her cart against her. Mother Courage of course makes no moral condemnation of Yvette and her special type of business.

## The colonel

The colonel whom Yvette lugs in to buy Courage's cart for her is difficult to play, because he is a purely negative quantity. His only function is to show the price the whore must pay for her rise in life; consequently he must be repellent. [Georg-Peter] Pilz portrayed the aged colonel subtly, making him mime an ardent passion of which he was not for one moment capable. The old man's lechery erupted as though in response to a cue, and he seemed to forget his surroundings. An instant later he forgot his lechery and stared absently into the void. The actor produced a striking effect with his stick. In his passionate moments he pressed it to the ground so hard that it bent; an instant later it snapped straight—this suggested loathsome aggressive impotence and produced an irresistibly comic effect. Considerable elegance is required to keep such a performance within the bounds of good taste.

## A detail

Having finished hanging up the washing, Kattrin stares open-mouthed at the visitors from the general's tent. The cook honours her with special attention as he follows Courage behind the cart. This is probably what gives her the idea of stealing Yvette's weapons.

## The two sides

While on one side of the cart the war is being discussed with frank mockery, Kattrin is appropriating some of the tools of the whore's trade and practising Yvette's swaying gait, which she has just seen. Here [Angelika] Hurwicz's facial expression was strained and deeply serious.

## 'A stronghold sure'

The first part of Kattrin's pantomime occurs after 'I wasn't mistaken in your face.' (The cook added: 'This is a war of faith.') At this point Courage, the cook and the chaplain placed themselves to one side of the cart in such a way that they could not see Kattrin, and struck up 'A stronghold sure'. They sang it with feeling, casting anxious glances around them as though such a song were illegal in the Swedish camp.

## The surprise attack

It must be brought out that Courage is used to such surprises and knows how to handle them. Before she thinks about saving the cannon, she rescues her washing. She helps the chaplain to disguise himself, she smears her daughter's face, she tells her son to throw the cash box away, she takes down the Swedish flag. All this she does as a matter of routine, but by no means calmly.
[ . . . ]

## The meal

Courage has prepared it. Enlarged by the new employee who was a chaplain only that morning, the little family still seem somewhat flurried; in talking they look around like prisoners, but the mother is making jokes again; the Catholics, she says, need trousers as much as the Protestants. They have not learned that honesty is just as mortally dangerous among Catholics as among Lutherans.

## The chaplain

The chaplain has found a refuge. He has his own bowl to eat from and he makes himself awkwardly useful, hauls buckets of water, scours knives, and so on. Otherwise he is still an outsider. For this reason or because of his phlegmatic disposition he shows no exaggerated involvement in the tragedy of the honest son. While Courage is engaged in her unduly prolonged bargaining, he looks upon her simply as his source of support.

## Swiss Cheese

It seems to be hard for an actor to repress his pity for the character he is playing and not to reveal his knowledge of his impending death. In speaking to his sister Swiss Cheese shows no forebodings; this is what makes him so moving when he is taken.

## Brother and sister

The short conversation between dumb Kattrin and Swiss Cheese is quiet and not without tenderness. Shortly before the destruction we are shown for the last time what is to be destroyed.

The scene goes back to an old Japanese play in which two boys conclude a friendship pact. Their way of doing this is that one shows the other a flying bird, while the second shows the first a cloud.

## A detail

Kattrin gesticulates too wildly in telling her mother about the arrest of Swiss Cheese. Consequently Courage does not understand her and says: 'Use your hands, I don't like it when you howl like a dog, what'll his reverence say? Makes him uncomfortable.' Hurwicz made Kattrin pull herself together and nod. She understands this argument, it is a strong one.

## A detail

While the sergeant was questioning her in the presence of Swiss Cheese, Courage rummaged in a basket—a busy business woman with no time for formalities. But after the sentence. 'And don't you twist his shoulder', she ran after the soldiers who were leading him away.

## Yvette's three trips

Yvette runs back and forth three times for the sake of Courage's son and her cart. Her anger changes from mere anger at Courage's attempt to swindle her by paying her out of the regimental cash box to anger at Courage's betrayal of her son.

### Kattrin and the bargaining over Swiss Cheese

The portrayal of dumb Kattrin is not realistic if her goodness is stressed to the point of making her oppose her mother's attempt to get the amount of the bribe reduced. She runs off from scouring the knives when she begins to see that the bargaining has been going on too long. When after the execution Yvette sends her ahead and she goes to her mother with her face averted, there may be a reproach in this—but above all she cannot look her in the face.

### The denial

Courage is sitting, holding the hand of her daughter who is standing. When the soldiers come in with the dead boy and she is asked to look at him, she stands up, goes over, looks at him, shakes her head, goes back and sits down. During all this she has an obstinate expression, her lower lip thrust forward. Here Weigel's recklessness in throwing away her role reaches its highest point.

(The actor playing the sergeant can command the spectator's astonishment by looking around at his men in astonishment at such hardness.)

### Observation

Her look of extreme suffering after she has heard the shots, her unscreaming open mouth and backward-bent head probably derived from a press photograph of an Indian woman crouched over the body of her dead son during the shelling of Singapore. Weigel must have seen it years before, though when questioned she did not remember it. That is how observations are stored up by actors. Actually it was only in the later performances that Weigel assumed this attitude.

[ ... ]

4

### THE SONG OF THE GRAND CAPITULATION.

*Mother Courage is sitting outside the captain's tent; she has come to put in a complaint about damage to her cart; a clerk advises her in vain to let well alone. A young soldier appears, also to make a complaint; she dissuades him. The bitter 'Song of the Grand Capitulation'.*

*Courage herself learns from the lesson she has given the young soldier
and leaves without having put in her complaint.*

## Overall arrangement

*Mother Courage is sitting outside the captain's tent; she has come to
put in a complaint about damage to her cart; a clerk advises her in
vain to let well alone. The clerk comes up to the bench where Courage
is sitting and speaks to her kindly. She remains obstinate.*

*A young soldier appears, also to make a complaint; she dissuades
him, arguing that his anger is too short. Two soldiers enter. The
younger wants to rush into the captain's tent and the older is holding
him back by main force. Courage intervenes and involves the young
man in a conversation about the danger of short attacks of anger.*

*The bitter 'Song of the Grand Capitulation'. The young soldier,
whose anger has evaporated, goes off cursing.*

*Courage herself learns from the lesson she has given the young sol-
dier, and leaves without putting in her complaint.*

## Courage's state of mind at the beginning of the scene

In the first rehearsals Weigel opened this scene in an attitude of dejection. This was not right.

Courage learns by teaching. She teaches capitulation and learns it.

The scene calls for bitterness at the start and dejection at the end.

## Courage's depravity

In no other scene is Courage so depraved as in this one, where she in-
structs the young man in capitulation to the higher-ups and then puts
her own teaching into effect. Nevertheless Weigel's face in this scene
shows a glimmer of wisdom and even of nobility, and that is good.
Because the depravity is not so much that of her person as that of her
class, and because she herself at least rises above it somewhat by
showing that she understands this weakness and that it even makes
her angry.

[ . . . ]

## The scene played without alienation

Such a scene is socially disastrous if by hypnotic action the actress
playing Mother Courage invites the audience to identify with her. This
will only increase the spectator's own tendencies to resignation and

capitulation—besides giving him the pleasure of being superior to himself. It will not put him in a position to feel the beauty and attraction of a social problem.

## 5

### MOTHER COURAGE LOSES FOUR OFFICERS' SHIRTS AND DUMB KATTRIN FINDS A BABY.

*After a battle. Courage refuses to give the chaplain her officers' shirts to bandage wounded peasants. Kattrin threatens her mother. At the risk of her life Kattrin saves an infant. Courage laments the loss of her shirts and snatches a stolen coat away from a soldier who has stolen some schnapps, while Kattrin rocks the baby in her arms.*

## Overall arrangement

*After a battle.* Courage is standing with two soldiers outside her cart; its sideboard is lowered for use as a bar. Kattrin, sitting on the steps, is uneasy. Courage gulps down two glasses of schnapps; she needs them to harden her to the sight of misery.

*Courage refuses to give the chaplain her officers' shirts to bandage wounded peasants.* From inside a peasant's wrecked house the chaplain shouts for linen. Kattrin is prevented by her mother from taking officers' shirts from the cart. Courage obstinately blocks the steps, letting no one in.

*Kattrin threatens her mother.* With the help of one soldier the chaplain has carried a wounded woman out of the house, then an old peasant whose arm is dangling. Again he calls for linen and all look at Courage who lapses into silence. Angrily Kattrin seizes a plank and threatens her mother. The chaplain has to take it away from her. He picks Courage up, sets her down on a chest, and takes some officers' shirts.

*At the risk of her life Kattrin saves an infant.* Still struggling with the chaplain, Courage sees her daughter rush into the house that is threatening to cave in, to save a baby. Tugged both ways, between Kattrin and the officers' shirts, she runs about until the shirts are torn into bandages and Kattin comes out of the house with the infant. Now she runs after Kattrin to make her get rid of the baby. (Movements: Kattrin with the baby runs counter-clockwise around the wounded, then clockwise around the cart.) Her mother stops in the middle of the stage because the chaplain is coming out of the cart with the shirts. Kattrin sits down on the chest right.

*Courage laments the loss of her shirts and snatches a stolen coat away from a soldier who has stolen some schnapps, while Kattrin rocks the baby in her arms.* After springing like a tigress at the soldier who has failed to pay, Mother Courage stuffs his fur coat into the cart.

## A new Courage

A change has taken place in Courage. She has sacrificed her son to the cart and now she defends the cart like a tigress. She has been hardened by the hard bargains she drives.

## A detail

At the beginning of the scene (after 'They give us victory marches all right, but catch them giving men their pay') Weigel's Courage tossed off two glasses of schnapps. Apart from this extenuating circumstance, she provided no justification for Courage's haggling, scolding and raging throughout the scene.

## A detail

There was a kind of by-play between the soldier who gets no schnapps from Courage and the soldier drinking schnapps at the bar. It expressed the hostility between the haves and the have-nots. The drinker grins scornfully and drains his glass with ostentatious enjoyment, the have-not gives him a long hostile stare before turning around in disgust and going defeated to the rear—to wait for a chance to lay hands on the schnapps. Later the drinker will show more sympathy than the thirsty man for the wounded peasant woman.

## The contradictions must not disappear

The character of the chaplain is based on a contradiction. He is part scoundrel, part superior intelligence. The actor [Werner] Hinz gave him a wooden, awkward, comical quality, which he retained in his role of good Samaritan. His manner was stiff and cold, as though it were only his clergyman's past that impelled him to turn against his present employer. But something else shone through: his former high position gives him the leadership on the battlefield where he acts in a spirit deriving from the realisation that in the last analysis he himself was one of the oppressed. When he helps the injured, it becomes clear that he too is to be pitied.

## The scene is dependent on mime

The effect of the battlefield scene depends entirely on the scrupulously detailed mime with which Kattrin shows her mounting anger at her mother's inhumanity. Angelika Hurwicz ran back and forth like an alarmed hen between the wounded peasants and Mother Courage. Up to the point when she began to argue, in gestures, with her mother, she made no attempt to repress the voluptuous curiosity that horror inspires in infantile persons. She carried the baby out of the house like a thief; at the end of the scene she lifted the baby up in the air, prodding it with both hands as though to make it laugh. If her mother's share in the spoils is the fur coat, hers is the baby.

## Kattrin

In the battlefield scene Kattrin threatens to kill her mother because she refuses the wounded peasants her linen. It is necessary to show an intelligent Kattrin from the start. (Her infirmity misleads actors into representing her as dull.) At the beginning she is fresh, gay and even-tempered—Hurwicz gave her a kind of awkward charm even in the conversation with her brother in scene 3. True, the helplessness of her tongue communicates itself to her body; but it is the war that breaks her, not her infirmity; in technical terms, the war must find something that remains to be broken.

The whole point is missed if her love of children is depreciated as mindless animal instinct. Her saving of the city of Halle is an intelligent act. How else would it be possible to bring out what must be brought out, namely, that here the most helpless creature of all is ready to help?

## A detail

At the end of the scene Kattrin lifted the baby into the air, while Courage rolled up the fur coat and threw it into the cart: both women had their share of the spoils.

## Music and pauses

Music played an essential part in the fifth (battlefield) scene.

Victory march: from the start to 'Somebody give me a hand'.

From after 'My arm's gone' to 'I can't give nowt'.

From after '. . . happy as a queen in all this misery' to the end of the scene.

Pauses after:

'Town must of paid him something.'

'Where's that linen?'

'Blood's coming through.' [This line spoken by the chaplain is deleted from the final text. It followed 'All your victories mean to me is losses.']

6

PROSPERITY HAS SET IN, BUT KATTRIN IS
DISFIGURED.

*Mother Courage, grown prosperous, is stocktaking; funeral oration for the fallen field marshal Tilly. Conversation about the duration of the war; the chaplain proves that the war is going to go on for a long time. Kattrin is sent to buy merchandise. Mother Courage declines a proposal of marriage and insists on firewood. Kattrin is permanently disfigured by some soldiers and rejects Yvette's red shoes. Mother Courage curses the war.*

## Overall arrangements

*Mother Courage, grown prosperous, is stocktaking; funeral oration for the fallen field marshal Tilly.* Courage interrupts her counting of merchandise to serve brandy to some soldiers who are playing hooky from the funeral. She virtuously reproves them, declaring that she feels sorry for generals because the common people don't give their grandiose plans proper support. Meanwhile she is looking for worms in a tin box. The regimental clerk listens in vain, hoping to catch her in a subversive utterance.

*Conversation about the duration of the war; the chaplain proves that the war will go on for a long time.* The right section of the stage is the private quarters. To the left are the bar and the guest table at which the clerk and the chaplain are sitting. There is by-play between right and left when the drinking soldier sings for Kattrin and she smiles at him, while Courage, with a bundle of belt buckles which she is counting, comes over to the table to ask the chaplain-potboy how long he thinks the war will go on. All through his cynical comments she stands deep in thought. Should she lay in new supplies?

*Kattrin is sent to buy merchandise.* When the chaplain-potboy says the war will go on for a long time, Kattrin runs angrily behind the cart. Courage laughs, brings her back and sends her to the camp with a big basket to buy merchandise. 'Don't let them take nowt, think of your dowry.'

*Mother Courage declines a proposal of marriage and insists on firewood.* Courage has sat down on a stool beside her cart; she fills a pipe and tells the potboy to chop some firewood. He chops clumsily, complaining that his talents are lying fallow, and, probably with a view to avoiding physical labour, asks her to marry him. She hints that she doesn't want to take anybody into her business, and leads him gently back to the chopping block.

*Kattrin is permanently disfigured by some soldiers and rejects Yvette's red shoes.* Kattrin staggers in with a basket full of merchandise. She collapses at the entrance to the tent and Courage has to drag her over to her stool and dress her wound. Kattrin rejects the red shoes that her mother brings out to comfort her; they are now useless. With silent reproach she crawls into the cart.

*Mother Courage curses the war.* Slowly Courage brings forward the new supplies, which Kattrin has defended at such cost, and gets down on her knees to look them over in the place where she was stocktaking at the beginning of the scene. She recognises that war is a miserable source of income and for the first and last time curses the war.

## Inventory

Again Courage has changed. Increasing prosperity has made her softer and more human. Both qualities attract the chaplain and he proposes to her. For the first time we see her sitting briefly at rest, not working.

## Funeral oration for Tilly

In the course of many performances it was found that Courage's funeral oration for the field marshal is more effective if during the pause, when all are looking to the rear and the funeral march has grown loud and solemn, the clerk, who is slightly tipsy, rises from his chair and watches Courage closely, suspecting that in this oration she is ridiculing the field marshal. He sits down again in disappointment, because Courage has not said anything demonstrably incriminating.

(The pause during the funeral march must be long; otherwise the funeral scene will not produce the right effect.)

## A detail

In the funeral oration for field marshal Tilly ('Can't help feeling sorry for those generals and emperors') Weigel added—after 'how's he to know any better?'—'Jesus Christ, the worms have got into my biscuits.' While saying this she laughed. Here Mother Courage releases the merriment which, with the clerk looking on, she was unable to express in her evasively subversive speech.

## Mime

The chaplain's remarks on the longevity of the war must not take on an independent existence. They are the answer to Courage's anxious question as to whether she can risk taking in new merchandise. While the chaplain was talking, Weigel mimed Courage's anxiety and calculations.

## A detail

The drunken soldier addresses his song to Kattrin. She smiles at him. For the last time before she is disfigured the spectator is reminded that she is capable of love.

## A point to consider

Violent occupations lead actors to shout. The actor playing the chaplain shouted occasionally while chopping wood. The scene suffered.
[ . . . ]

## Kattrin

Again sitting huddled on the chest as during the drunken soldier's song, the injured girl merely touches her forehead gingerly once or twice to make sure where the wound is; otherwise, except for the willingness with which she lets herself be bandaged, she gives no indication of knowing what the scar will mean to her. Protest is expressed by her lack of interest in Yvette's red shoes and by the way she crawls into the cart: she blames her mother for what has happened to her.

## Contradiction

Courage has cursed the war while gathering up the supplies in defence of which her daughter has been disfigured.

Resuming the stocktaking begun at the start of the scene, she now counts the new articles.

# 7

## MOTHER COURAGE AT THE PEAK OF HER BUSINESS CAREER.

*Mother Courage has corrected her opinion of the war and sings its praises as a good provider.*

## Overall arrangement

*Mother Courage has corrected her opinion of the war and sings its praises as a good provider.* Pulled by Kattrin and the chaplain-potboy, the cart comes in from the rear and rolls along the footlights. Courage walks beside them, arguing with them; then, while singing, she turns to the audience. Pause.

## Signs of prosperity

After some forty performances it seemed to us that in scene 6, for the stocktaking, Courage should have rings on her fingers and a chain of silver talers round her neck as a sign of the relative prosperity she had achieved. But after a few more performances one of us discovered that this weakened her speech about the courage of the poor, and we decided to put the signs of prosperity in scene 7. Here, where she retracts her condemnation of war, her recently acquired signs of prosperity show her up for what she is: bribed.

In this short scene Weigel showed Courage in the full possession of her vitality, as previously only in scene 5 (the battlefield scene); in scene 5, however, she was gloomy; here she was cheerful.
[ . . . ]

8

## PEACE THREATENS TO RUIN MOTHER COURAGE'S BUSINESS. HER DASHING SON PERFORMS ONE HEROIC DEED TOO MANY AND COMES TO A STICKY END.

*Courage and the chaplain hear a rumour that peace has broken out. The cook reappears. The fight for the feedbag. An old friend who has made a good thing of the war; Puffing Piet is unmasked. The downfall of Eilif, Mother Courage's dashing son; he is executed for one of the misdeeds that had brought him rewards during the war. The peace comes to an end; Courage leaves the chaplain and goes on with the cook in the wake of the Swedish army.*

### Overall arrangement

*Courage and the chaplain hear a rumour that peace has broken out.* On the right stand an old woman and her son who have come from the city with all sorts of household goods to sell. It is early in the morning, and Courage, still half asleep, answers sulkily from the cart left. Then bells are heard from the right, the chaplain crawls out from under the cart where he has been sleeping and Courage sticks her head out of the cart. The bells seem to have made the old woman happy—not so Mother Courage.

*The cook reappears.* The bells of peace bring all sorts of visitors. First comes—from the right like the rest—the cook, ragged, with all his possessions in a bundle. The chaplain is not pleased to see him, but Courage, who is braiding her hair, runs out to meet him and shakes his hand heartily. She invites him over to a wooden bench in front of the cart, while the chaplain goes behind the cart to put on his clerical garb. Amid the ringing of the bells they sit there almost like lovers, telling each other about the bankruptcy that peace has brought them.

*The fight for the feedbag.* When the chaplain comes back—he stands in the middle of the stage like a last incisor in a toothless mouth—the cook begins to demolish him. Courage climbs into her cart to get her pack ready; she is going to sell the merchandise she bought when the chaplain promised her a long war. The cook starts unwrapping his feet because he means to stay, and the chaplain is obliged to beg him humbly not to drive him out. The cook merely shrugs his shoulders.

*An old friend who has made a good thing of the war; Puffing Piet is unmasked.* Another visitor. Fat and asthmatic, walking with the help of a cane, the Countess Starhemberg, the former camp whore, enters, clothed in black silk and followed by a servant. She has dismounted from her carriage to call on Mother Courage. She catches sight of the cook, known to her as Puffing Piet, and angrily denounces him to Courage, who has difficulty in preventing her from attacking him with her cane.

*The downfall of Eilif, Mother Courage's dashing son; he is executed for one of the misdeeds that brought him rewards during the war.* When the women have left, the cook gloomily puts his foot wrappings on again and the chaplain relishes his triumph. Their conversation turns to melancholy recollections of the good old war days. Blown in by the bells of peace, soldiers with harquebuses bring in a richly dressed lieutenant— Eilif. His courage deserts him when he hears that his mother is not there. The chaplain gives him a swallow of brandy and, a clergyman once again, accompanies him to the place of execution.

*The peace comes to an end; Courage goes on with the cook, in the wake of the Swedish army.* The cook tries to get Kattrin to come out of the cart so he can beg some bread from her. Courage comes running in, overjoyed. The peace is over. The cook does not mention Eilif's death. With the cook's help she packs her belongings into the cart and they go on without the chaplain.

## Advance preparation

In her conversation with the chaplain in scene 6 Weigel very carefully laid the groundwork for her conversation with the cook in scene 8. She said 'Nice fellow that' a little more warmly and thoughtfully than required by her good-natured rebuff of the chaplain. Consequently in scene 8 she had an audience who knew what was what. This enabled her to take a dry, matter-of-fact tone with the cook. Knowing what it knew, the audience could be touched as well as amused that the subject of their love dialogue should be the fact that they were both ruined.

## The dignity of misery

In the cockfight between the chaplain and the cook, Hinz as the chaplain obtained a powerful and natural effect when, suddenly throwing all arrogance to the winds, he begged the cook not to squeeze him out of his place with Courage because, having become a better man, he could no longer practise the clergyman's profession. His fear of losing his job lent him a new dignity. ·

## Humiliations

The cook too is capable of enduring humiliations. At the end of the dialogue in which he triumphs over the chaplain, he removes his shoes and foot wrappings like a man who has come to the end and goal of a long peregrination. Yvette finds him barefooted, which embarrasses the ageing Don Juan. After he has been unmasked and the chaplain has lectured him, he sorrowfully puts his footwear back on. The episode in which he begs Kattrin for food was played brilliantly by Bildt. His bundle slung over his shoulder, ready to hit the road, he first tapped his stick nonchalantly on the drum hanging from the cart. Talking into the cart, he uttered the words 'pork' and 'bread' in the tone of a gourmet and connoisseur: the starving cook.

## Good business

Yvette Pottier is the only character in the play who strikes it rich; she has sold herself for a good price. She has been as badly disfigured by good food as Kattrin by her scar; she is so fat one has the impression that eating has become her only passion. She speaks with the accent of the Austrian aristocracy.

[ . . . ]

## War the provider

Courage comes back from the village exhausted from running but overjoyed that the war has started up again. In high spirits she lets the cook relieve her of her pack. The prospect of good business will enable her to take the cook in. She speaks light-heartedly of the possibility of seeing her son again. 'Now there's war again, everything will work out all right' [not in the final text]. She is going to ride over his grave.

## A detail

While they are packing, Kattrin appears. She sees the cook staring at her scar, covers it with her hand and turns away. She has come to fear the light.

Again in scene 11, when the soldiers drag her out of the cart, she holds her hand over her eye.

9

## TIMES ARE HARD, THE WAR IS GOING BADLY. ON ACCOUNT OF HER DAUGHTER, SHE REFUSES THE OFFER OF A HOME.

*The cook has inherited a tavern in Utrecht. Kattrin hears the cook refuse to take her along there. The 'Song of the Temptations of the Great'. Kattrin decides to spare her mother the need to make a decision, packs her bundle and leaves a message. Mother Courage stops Kattrin from running away and goes on alone with her. The cook goes to Utrecht.*

### Overall arrangement

*Times are hard. The cook has inherited a tavern in Utrecht.* In the early dawn of a stormy winter day Courage and the cook, both in rags, bring the cart to a stop outside a parsonage. The cook morosely unharnesses himself and admits to Courage that he means to go to Utrecht where he has inherited a tavern. He asks her to go with him. Sitting shivering on the shaft, Courage complains of the bad business situation: the war is no longer finding much to feed on.

*Kattrin hears the cook refuse to take her along there.* The cook interrupts the conversation between mother and daughter about the peaceful life in Utrecht, and motions Courage to step to one side with him (to the right, in front of the parsonage). Hidden beside the cart, Kattrin hears the cook refuse to take her along.

*The cook and Courage sing the 'Song of the Temptations of the Great'.* While they sing their begging song, Courage desperately thinks over the cook's offer, presumably her last hope of settling down.

*Kattrin decides to spare her mother the need to make a decision, packs her bundle and leaves a message.* By the end of the begging song, Courage has made up her mind to decline the offer. She still goes into the parsonage with the cook for the sake of the soup. Kattrin comes in with a bundle and deposits her mother's skirt with the cook's trousers over it on the cart's shaft.

*Mother Courage stops Kattrin from running away and goes on alone with her.* Courage catches Kattrin just as she is about to steal away. She has brought a dish of soup. Feeding her as one would a child, she assures her that it has never occurred to her to desert the cart. She throws the cook's bundle and trousers out of the cart, puts herself and Kattrin in harness and starts off with her (behind the house, to the right).

*The cook goes to Utrecht.* The cook sees that the women and cart are gone. He silently picks up his bundle and sets out on his way, right rear, to settle down in Utrecht.

## The cook

In this scene the cook must not under any circumstances be represented as brutal. The tavern he has inherited is too small to keep three people, and the customers cannot be expected to put up with the sight of the disfigured Kattrin. That's all there is to it. Courage does not find his arguments unreasonable. Weigel showed plainly that Courage thought the proposition over—she thinks every proposition over. This she did by looking over towards the cart during the first stanza of the begging song with an expression compounded of indecision, fear and pity.
[ . . . ]

## A detail

In this scene, in which her arguments are rather thin, Courage speaks to her daughter as one speaks to a person who is hard of hearing. Her loud, slow delivery also gives the impression that she is speaking in the name of the cook as well, but without being at all sure of herself in this.

## Kattrin's demonstration

In laying out the trousers and skirt Kattrin tries to leave her mother a message explaining why she has gone away. But Hurwicz also indicated a note of resentment by glancing at the parsonage where her mother and the cook were presumably eating soup, then looking at her composition and stifling an uncanny, malignant giggle by raising her hand to her mouth before sneaking away.

## A detail

While saying the words 'Don't you go thinking it's on your account I gave him the push', Courage put a spoonful of soup into Kattrin's mouth.
[ . . . ]

## The cook sets out for Utrecht

Scenes of this kind must be fully acted out: Courage and Kattrin harness themselves to the cart, push it back a few feet so as to be able to circle the parsonage, and then move off to the right. The cook comes out, still chewing a piece of bread, sees his belongings, picks them up and goes off to the rear with long steps. We see him disappear. Thus the parting of the ways is made visible.

## 10

### STILL ON THE ROAD.

*Mother and daughter hear someone in a peasant house singing the 'Song of Home'.*

### The song in the Munich production

A fine variation used in the Munich production: the song was sung with unfeeling, provocative self-assurance. The arrogant pride of possession expressed in the singing turned the listeners on the road into damned souls.

### Expression not wanted

The two women enter, pulling the cart. They hear the voice from the peasant house, stop, listen, and start off again. What goes on in their minds should not be shown; the audience can imagine.

### A detail

In one of the later performances Weigel, when starting off again, tossed her head and shook it like a tired cart horse getting back to work. It is doubtful whether this gesture can be imitated.

## 11

### DUMB KATTRIN SAVES THE CITY OF HALLE.

*A surprise attack is planned on the city of Halle; soldiers force a young peasant to show them the way. The peasant and his wife tell Kattrin to join them in praying for the city. Kattrin climbs up on the barn roof and beats the drum to awaken the city. Neither the offer to spare her mother in the city nor the threat to smash the cart can make her stop drumming. Death of dumb Kattrin.*

## Overall arrangement

*A surprise attack is planned on the city of Halle; soldiers force a young peasant to show them the way.* An ensign and two soldiers come to a farm at night. They drag the peasants, still half asleep, out of the house and Kattrin out of her cart. By threatening to kill the peasants' only ox they force the young peasant to serve as their guide. (They lead him to the rear; the party go out right.)

*The peasant and his wife tell Kattrin to join them in praying for the city.* The peasant moves a ladder over to the barn (right), climbs up and sees that the woods are swarming with armed men. He comes down, he and his wife talk it over and decide not to endanger themselves by trying to warn the city. The peasant woman goes over to Kattrin (right front) and tells her to pray God to help the city. The three of them kneel down and pray.

*Kattrin climbs up on the barn roof and beats the drum to awaken the city.* From the peasant woman's prayer Kattrin learns that the children in Halle are in danger. Stealthily she takes the drum from the cart, the same drum she had brought back when she was disfigured. With it she climbs up on the barn roof. She starts drumming. The peasants try in vain to make her stop.

*Neither the offer to spare her mother in the city nor the threat to smash the cart can make her stop drumming.* At the sound of the drum the ensign and the soldiers come back with the young peasant. The soldiers take up a position by the cart and the ensign threatens the peasants with his sword. First one of the soldiers, then the ensign moves to the centre to make promises to Kattrin. The peasant goes over to a log (left front) and chops at it with an axe to drown out the sound of the drum. Kattrin is victorious in the noise contest, the ensign starts to go into the house to set it on fire, the peasant woman indicates the cart. One of the soldiers kicks the young peasant and forces him to batter the cart with a plank, the other soldier is sent off for an harquebus. He sets up the harquebus, the ensign orders him to fire.

*Kattrin's death.* Kattrin falls forward, the drumsticks in her drooping hands strike one full beat followed by a feeble beat; for a moment the ensign is triumphant, then the cannon of Halle responds, taking up the rhythm of Kattrin's drumbeats.

## Bad comedians are always laughing
## Bad tragedians are always weeping

In sad scenes just as in comic ones precision must be combined with ease; the hand that guides the arrangement must be both firm and relaxed. The actors take their positions and form their groups in very much the same way as the marbles tossed into a wooden bowl in certain roulette-like children's games fall into hollows, with the difference that in the games it is not decided in advance which marbles will fall into which hollows, whereas in theatrical arrangements there only seems to be no advance decision. And indeed the reason for the stiffness or heaviness that is so characteristic of sad scenes in the German theatre is that in tragedy the human body is unjustifiably neglected and so seems to be afflicted with muscular cramp. Which is deplorable.

## Kattrin's two fears

Kattrin's dumbness does not save her. The war gives her a drum. With this unsold drum she must climb up on the barn roof and save the children of Halle.

Conventional heroism must be avoided. Kattrin is ridden by two fears: her fear for the city of Halle and her fear for herself.

## 'The dramatic scene'

Audiences were especially stirred by the drum scene. Some explained this by saying that it is the most dramatic scene in the play and that the public likes its theatre dramatic rather than epic. In reality the epic theatre, while capable of portraying other things than stirring incidents, clashes, conspiracies, psychological torments and so on, is also capable of portraying these. Spectators may identify themselves with Kattrin in this scene; empathy may give them the happy feeling that they too possess such strength. But they are not likely to have experienced such empathy throughout the play —in the first scenes, for example.

## Alienation

If the scene is to be saved from a wild excitement amid which everything worth noticing is lost, close attention must be given to alienation.

For example: if the conversation of the peasants is swallowed up by a general hubbub, the audience will be in danger of being 'carried away'; then they will fail to take note how the peasants justify their failure to act, how they fortify each other in the belief that there is nothing they can do, so that the only remaining possibility of 'action' becomes prayer.

In view of this, the actors in rehearsal were made to add 'said the man' or 'said the woman' after each speech. For example:

' "Sentries are bound to spot them first," said the woman.'
' "Sentry must have been killed," said the man.'
' "If only there were more of us," said the woman.'
' "Just you and me and that cripple," said the man.'
' "Nowt we can do, you'd say . . ." said the woman.'
' "Nowt," said the man,' and so on.

### Kattrin's drumming

Kattrin keeps watching what is going on down below. Consequently her drumming breaks off after the following sentences,

'Jesus Christ, what's she doing?'
'I'll cut you all to ribbons!'
'We got a suggestion could do you some good.'
'With a mug like yours it's not surprising.'
'We must set the farm on fire.'

### Detail in tempestuous scenes

Such scenes as the one where the peasant tries to drown the noise of Kattrin's drumming by chopping wood must be fully acted out. As she drums, Kattrin must look down at the peasant and accept the challenge. In tempestuous scenes the director needs a certain amount of stubbornness to make miming of this sort last long enough.

### A detail

Hurwicz showed increasing exhaustion while drumming.

### The ritual character of despair

The lamentations of the peasant woman, whose son the soldiers have taken away and whose farm they threaten when Kattrin starts her drumming to wake the townspeople, must have a certain routine quality about it; it must suggest a 'set behaviour pattern'. The war has been going on too long. Begging, lamenting, and informing have frozen into fixed forms: they are the things you do when the soldiery arrive.

It is worth forgoing the 'immediate impression' of a particular, seemingly unique episode of horror so as to penetrate a deeper stratum of horror and to show how repeated, constantly recurring misfortune has driven people to ritualise their gestures of self-defence—though of course these ritual gestures can never free them from the reality of fear, which on the stage must permeate the ritual.

[ . . . ]

## 12

### MOTHER COURAGE MOVES ON.

*The peasants have to convince Courage that Kattrin is dead. The lullaby for Kattrin. Mother Courage pays for Kattrin's burial and receives the condolences of the peasants. Alone, Mother Courage harnesses herself to the empty cart; still hoping to get back into business, she follows the ragged army.*

### Overall arrangement

*The peasants have to convince Courage that Kattrin is dead.* The cart is standing on the empty stage. Mother Courage is sitting with the dead Kattrin's head in her lap. The peasants are standing in a hostile knot at the dead girl's feet. Courage speaks as if her daughter were only sleeping, deliberately disregarding the reproaches of the peasants who are saying that she is to blame for Kattrin's death.

*The lullaby for Kattrin.* The mother's face is bent low over her daughter's face. Her song fails to pacify the peasants.

*Mother Courage pays for Kattrin's burial and receives the condolences of the peasants.* When she realises that her last child is dead, she rises painfully to her feet and hobbles around the corpse (on the right) and along the footlights to behind the cart. She comes back with a sheet of canvas. The peasants ask her if she has no one else; she answers over her shoulder: 'Aye, one left. Eilif.' And with her back to the audience she lays the canvas over the body. Then at the head end of the body she pulls it up over the face and stands behind the body, facing the audience. The peasant and his son give her their hands and bow ceremoniously before carrying the body away (to the right). The woman also gives Courage her hand, goes to the right and stops again in indecision. The women exchange a few words, then the peasant woman goes away.

*Alone, Mother Courage harnesses herself to her empty cart; still*

*hoping to get back into business, she follows the ragged army.* Slowly
the old woman goes to the cart, unrolls the cord which Kattrin had until then been pulling, takes a stick, examines it, pulls the loop of the
second cord through, wedges the stick under her arm and moves off.
The last stanza of the 'Mother Courage Song' has begun as she is
bending down over the shaft. The revolve begins to turn and Mother
Courage circles the stage once. The curtain falls as she turns right rear
for the second time.

### The peasants

The peasants' attitude towards Courage is hostile. She has caused them
great difficulties and they will have her on their hands if she cannot
catch up with the departing army. As they see it, she is to blame for
what has happened. Besides, she is an unsedentary element, and now
in wartime belongs with the incendiaries, cutthroats and looters who
follow in the wake of armies. In condoling with her by giving her their
hands, they are only doing what is customary.

### The bow

During the whole scene Weigel showed an almost bestial stupor. All
the more beautiful was her deep bow when the body was carried away.

### The lullaby

The lullaby must be sung without any sentimentality or desire to provoke sentimentality. Otherwise its significance is lost. The idea under-
lying this song is murderous: this mother's child must fare better than
other children of other mothers. By slight emphasis on the 'you',
Weigel portrayed Courage's treacherous hope of bringing her child,
and perhaps hers alone, through the war. To this child who had
lacked even the most ordinary things, she promised the most extraordinary.

### Paying for the burial

Even in paying for the burial, Weigel gave one last hint of Courage's
character. She fished a few coins out of her leather bag, put one back
and gave the peasants the rest. This did not in the least detract from
the overpowering effect of desolation.

## The last stanza

The last stanza of the 'Mother Courage Song' was struck up by the musicians in the box while Courage was slowly harnessing herself to the cart. It gives powerful expression to her still unshattered hope of getting her cut from the war. It gains in power if the illusion that the song is being sung by marching armies in the distance is dropped.
[ . . . ]

## Timing

At the end as at the beginning the cart must be seen rolling along. Of course the audience would understand if it were simply pulled away. When it goes on rolling there is a moment of irritation ('this has been going on long enough'). But when it goes on still longer, a deeper understanding sets in.

## The pulling of the cart in the last scene

For scene 12 the peasants' house and the barn with roof (from scene 11) were removed from the stage; only the cart and Kattrin's body remained. The word 'Saxony' in big letters is hoisted into the flies when the music starts. Thus the cart was hauled off a completely empty stage recalling scene 1. Mother Courage described a complete circle with it on the revolving stage, passing the footlights for the last time. As usual, the stage was brilliantly lit.

## Realist discoveries

In giving the peasants the money for Kattrin's burial, Weigel quite mechanically puts back one of the coins she has taken out of her purse. What does this gesture accomplish? It shows that in all her grief the business woman has not wholly forgotten how to reckon— money is hard to come by. This little gesture has the power and suddenness of a discovery—a discovery concerning human nature, which is moulded by conditions. To dig out the truth from the rubble of the self-evident, to link the particular strikingly with the universal, to capture the particular that characterises a general process, that is the art of the realist.

## A change in the text

After 'I'll manage, there isn't much in it', Courage added, first in the Munich, then in the Berlin production: 'I've got to get back into business.'

## Mother Courage learns nothing

In the last scene Weigel's Courage seemed to be eighty years old. And she understands nothing. She reacts only to remarks connected with the war, such as that she mustn't be left behind, and takes no notice when the peasants brutally accuse her of being to blame for Kattrin's death.

In 1938, when the play was written, Courage's inability to learn from war's unprofitable character was a prophecy. At the time of the 1948 Berlin production the wish was expressed that at least in the play Courage would understand.

In order that the realism of this play should benefit the spectator, that is, in order that the spectator should learn something, the theatre must work out a way of playing it which does not lead to audience identification with the principal character (heroine).

To judge by press reviews and statements of spectators, the original production in Zürich, for example, though artistically on a high level, merely pictured war as a natural catastrophe and ineluctable fate, confirming the belief of the petit-bourgeois members of the audience in their own indestructibility and power to survive. But even for the equally petit-bourgeois Mother Courage the decision whether or not to join in was left open throughout the play. It follows that the production must have represented Courage's business activity, her desire to get her cut and her willingness to take risks, as perfectly natural and 'eternally human' phenomena, so that there was no way out. Today the petit-bourgeois can no longer in fact keep out of the war, as Courage could have done. And probably no performance of the play can give a petit-bourgeois anything more than a real horror of war and a certain insight into the fact that the big business deals which constitute war are not made by the little people. A play is more instructive than reality, because in it the war situation is set up experimentally for the purpose of giving insight; that is, the spectator assumes the attitude of a student—provided the production is right. The proletarians in the audience, the members of a class which really can take action against war and eliminate it, must be given an insight—which of course is possible only if the play is performed in the right way—into the connection between war and commerce: the proletariat as a class can do away with war by doing away with capitalism. Here, of course, a good deal depends on the growth of self-awareness among the proletariat, a process that is going on both inside and outside the theatre.

## The epic element

As for the epic element in the Deutsches Theater production, indications of it could be seen in the arrangement, in the delineation of the characters, in the accurate execution of detail, and in the spirited rhythm of the entire performance. Moreover, the contradictions that pervade the play were not taken over ready-made, but worked out, and the parts, visible as such, fitted well into the whole. Nonetheless, the central aim of the epic theatre was not achieved. Much was shown, but the element of showing was absent. Only in a few rehearsals devoted to recasting was it brought out clearly. Here the actors 'marked', that is, they merely showed the new members of the cast certain positions and tones, and the whole took on the wonderfully relaxed, effortless, and unobtrusive quality that stimulates the spectator to think and feel for himself.

No one missed this fundamental epic element; and this is probably why the actors did not dare to provide it.

## Concerning these notes

It is to be hoped that the present notes, indicating a few of the ideas and devices of various kinds that are necessary for the performance of a play, will not make an impression of misplaced seriousness. It is difficult in writing about these things to convey the carefree lightness that is essential to the theatre. Even in their instructive aspect, the arts belong to the realm of entertainment.

[From *Mutter Courage und ihre Kinder. Text/Aufführung/ Anmerkungen*. Henschel-Verlag, East Berlin, 1956.]

## TWO WAYS OF PLAYING MOTHER COURAGE

When the title role is played in the usual way, so as to communicate empathy, the spectator (according to numerous witnesses) experiences an extraordinary pleasure: the indestructible vitality of this woman beset by the hardships of war leaves him with a sense of triumph. Mother Courage's active participation in the war is not taken seriously; the war is a source, perhaps her only source, of livelihood. Apart from this element of participation, in spite of it, the effect is very much as in

*Schweyk*, where—in a comic perspective, to be sure—the audience triumphs with Schweyk over the plans of the belligerent powers to sacrifice him. But in the case of Mother Courage such an effect has far less social value, precisely because her participation, however indirect it may seem, is not taken into consideration. The effect is indeed negative. Courage is represented chiefly as a mother, and like Niobe she is unable to protect her children against fate—in this case, war. At most, her merchant's trade and the way she plies it give her a 'realistic, un-ideal' quality; they do not prevent the war from being seen as fate. It remains, of course, wholly evil, but after all she comes through it alive, though deformed. By contrast Weigel, employing a technique which prevents complete empathy, treated the merchant's trade not as a natural but as a historical one—that is, belonging to a historical, *transient* period—and war as the best time for it. Here too the war was a self-evident source of livelihood, but this spring from which Mother Courage drank death was a polluted one. The merchant-mother became a great living contradiction, and it was this contradiction which utterly disfigured and deformed her. In the battlefield scene, which is cut in most productions, she really was a hyaena; she parted with the shirts because she saw her daughter's hatred and feared violence; she cursed at the soldier with the coat and pounced on him like a tigress. When her daughter was disfigured, she cursed the war with the same profound sincerity that characterised her praise of it in the scene immediately following. Thus she played the contradictions in all their irreconcilable sharpness. Her daughter's rebellion against her (when the city of Halle is saved) stunned her completely and taught her nothing. The tragedy of Mother Courage and of her life, which the audience was made to feel deeply, lay in a terrible contradiction which destroyed a human being, a contradiction which has been transcended, but only by society itself in long and terrible struggles. What made this way of playing the part morally superior was that human beings—even the strongest of them—were shown to be destructible.

[Written 1951. From GW *Schriften zum Theater*, p. 895. First published in *Theaterarbeit*, 1952.]

# MISFORTUNE IN ITSELF IS A POOR TEACHER

The audience gave off the acrid smell of clothing that had not been properly cleaned, but this did not detract from the festive atmosphere. Those who had come to see the play had come from ruins and would be going back to ruins. There was more light on the stage than on any square or in any house.

The wise old stage manager from the days of Max Reinhardt had received me like a king, but what gave the production its hard realism was a bitter experience shared by all. The dressmakers in the workshops realised that the costumes had to be richer at the beginning of the play than at the end. The stage hands knew how the canvas over Mother Courage's cart had to be: white and new at the beginning, then dirty and patched, then somewhat cleaner, but never again really white, and at the end a rag.

Weigel's way of playing Mother Courage was hard and angry; that is, her Mother Courage was not angry; she herself, the actress, was angry. She showed a merchant, a strong crafty woman who loses her children to the war one after another and still goes on believing in the profit to be derived from war.

A number of people remarked at the time that Mother Courage learns nothing from her misery, that even at the end she does not *understand*. Few realised that just this was the bitterest and most meaningful lesson of the play.

Undoubtedly the play was a great success; that is, it made a big impression. People pointed out Weigel on the street and said: 'Mother Courage!' But I do not believe, and I did not believe at the time, that the people of Berlin—or of any other city where the play was shown—understood the play. They were all convinced that they had learned something from the war; what they failed to grasp was that, in the playwright's view, Mother Courage was meant to have learned nothing from her war. They did not see what the playwright was driving at: that war teaches people nothing.

Misfortune in itself is a poor teacher. Its pupils learn hunger and thirst, but seldom hunger for truth or thirst for knowledge. Suffering does not transform a sick man into a physician. Neither what he sees from a distance nor what he sees face to face is enough to turn an eyewitness into an expert.

The audiences of 1949 and the ensuing years did not see Mother Courage's crimes, her participation, her desire to share in the profits of the war business; they saw only her failure, her sufferings. And that was their view of Hitler's war in which they had participated: it had been a bad war and now they were suffering. In short, it was exactly as the playwright had prophesied. War would bring them not only suffering, but also the inability to learn from it.

The production of *Mother Courage and Her Children* is now in its sixth year. It is certainly a brilliant production, with great actors.

Undoubtedly something has changed. The play is no longer a play that came too late, that is, *after* a war. Today a new war is threatening with all its horrors. No one speaks of it, but everyone knows. The masses are not in favour of war. But life is so full of hardships. Mightn't war do away with these? Didn't people make a very good living in the last war, at any rate till just before the end? And aren't there such things as successful wars?

I am curious to know how many of those who see *Mother Courage and Her Children* today understand its warning.

[Written 1954. From GW *Schriften zum Theater*, p. 1147.]

# Editorial Notes

The first typescript of *Mother Courage*, in Brecht's own typing with its characteristic absence of capital letters, was made in 1939, though there is also what may be a slightly earlier draft of the first few pages in verse. Amended by Brecht and by his collaborator Margarete Steffin, who died in 1941, it was then duplicated for the Zürich production and again in 1946 by the Kurt Reiss agency in Basel. This seems to have been the text which Brecht circulated to some of his friends, and of which one scene was accordingly published in the Moscow *Internationale Literatur* before the première, while a copy served as the basis for H. R. Hays's first American translation. Brecht made a few further additions and alterations to the 1946 version, which was once again duplicated for the Deutsches Theater production of 1949. Brecht's own copies of this Deutsches Theater script bear yet more notes and small amendments, as well as cuts which were disregarded in the published version. This appeared as *Versuche* 9 in 1949, continuing the grey paperbound series of Brecht's writings which had been interrupted in 1933.

The main shifts of emphasis in the play were indicated by Brecht in his own notes which followed the first publication of the play in the *Versuche* (1949) and have been reprinted in subsequent editions (pp. 85–138 here). The final versions of these passages, with the exception of the last (which concludes the play) are to be found in the additions to the Deutsches Theater typescript. The change in scene 1, says Brecht's diary, was proposed by his assistant Kuckhahn. In the case of the last scene, the major change took place subsequently, between the *Versuche* edition of 1949 and the reprint of 1950. It consisted in the insertion of the stage directions showing Mother Courage first covering her daughter's body, then handing over money to the peasants who carry it away, and of the last sentence 'Have to get back in business again.' In previous versions, too, she was made to join in the refrain of the final song. Now, presumably, she was too old and exhausted to do more than pull her cart.

These changes were, as Brecht said, calculated to bring out Courage's short-sighted concentration on business and alienate the audience's sympathies. Thus in scene 1 she now became distracted by the chance of selling a belt buckle; in scene 5 she no longer helped the others to make bandages of her expensive shirts; while in scene 7 she was shown prospering (her lines up to 'Them as does are the first to go' were new, while the scene title 'Mother Courage at the peak of her business career' and the silver necklace of the stage direction were added after the 1949 edition). Besides these, however, Brecht made earlier alterations to two of the main characters—the cook and the camp prostitute Yvette—and to virtually all the songs, whose independent role in the play became considerably strengthened as a result. Scene 8 seems to have called for repeated amendment, thanks partly to Brecht's uncertainty about the Yvette–cook relationship, which in turn depended on the choice of song for scene 3, where it is first expressed. Another confusion which has perhaps left its mark on the final text concerns religion: the first typescript gave the chaplain the Catholic title of 'Kaplan' throughout, putting Courage initially in the Catholic camp, which the Lutherans then overran in scene 3. Though Brecht corrected this on the script, to conform with the rest of the story, the religious antagonism emerges none too clearly even in the final version.

Brecht's first typescript also numbered the scenes rather differently, so as to run from 1 to 11, omitting the present scenes 7 and 10. He altered this to make 9 scenes, a division which he retained in the 1946 script, writing the original scene titles, to correspond with it, very nearly in their present form. 'The Story' (pp. 88–90 here) refers to this numbering, as also does a note attached to the typescript:

> The minor parts can easily be divided among a small number of actors. For instance the sergeant in scene 1 can also play the wounded peasant in scene 5 and the young man in scene 7 [8]; the general in scene 2 can be the clerk in scene 4 and the old peasant in scene 9 [11], and so on. Moreover the soldier in scene 3, the young soldier in scene 4 and the ensign in scene 9 [11] can be performed by the same actor without alteration of makeup.

## SETTINGS AND COSTUMES

High road with a Swedish city in the background/Inside the general's tent/Camp/Outside an officer's tent/In a bombarded village/In a canteen tent during rain/In the woods outside a city/Outside a parsonage in the winter/Near a thatched peasant dwelling.

The chief item of scenery consists of Courage's cart, from which one must be able to deduce her current financial situation. The brief scenes on the high road which are appended to scenes 6 and 8 [now scenes 7 and 10] can be played in front of the curtain.

So far as the costumes are concerned, care must be taken to avoid the brand-new elegance common in historical plays. They must show the poverty involved in a long war.

The following scene-by-scene résumé of the changes follows the same numbering, the present scene numbers being given in square brackets.

1. [1]
In Brecht's first typescript the family arrive to the sound of a piano-accordion, not a Jew's harp, and there are some minor differences in the Mother Courage song.

2. [2]
The cook's original name 'Feilinger' is amended to 'Lamb' on the first typescript. The general's reference to the king and Eilif's reply were added to this; the general's following 'You've got something in common already' was an afterthought added on the Deutsches Theater script (according to Manfred Wekwerth it was meant to refer to the enthusiasm with which Eilif drank). Eilif's *dancing a war dance with his sabre* was penned by Brecht on the 1946 script.

The song itself is taken over from Brecht's first collection of poems, *Die Hauspostille* (1927), and derives originally from the verse at the end of Kipling's short story *Love o' Women*, itself taken from the song of the Girl and the Soldier in the story *My Great and Only*.

3. [3]
The three sub-scenes (divided by the passage of time) are numbered 3, 3a and 3b, of which only the first has a title. Yvette originally was Jessie Potter, amended on the first typescript to Jeannette Pottier; she had become Yvette by 1946. The scene started with Mother Courage's remark to Swiss Cheese 'Here's your woollies,' everything to do with the armourer being added to the first typescript (p. 19).

Instead of the 'Song of Fraternisation', Jessie *sings the song of Surabaya-Johnny* (from *Happy End*), immediately after the words 'Then I'll tell you, get it off my chest', Courage having just said 'Just don't start in on your Johnny.' The text of this song is not reproduced in the typescript, but a first version of Johnny's description is inserted, with Jeannette 'growing up on Batavia' and the man being a 'ship's cook, blond, a Swede, but skinny'. In pen, Batavia is changed to Flanders, ship's cook to army cook and Swede to Dutchman. A 'Song of Pipe-and-Drum Henny' is added, which is a slightly adapted version of 'Surabaya-Johnny' in three verses (the refrain appears only in the 1946 script). In the text of this song, which still fits the Weill music, Burma is amended to Utrecht and the fish market (in 'You were something to do with the fish market / And nothing to do with the army') to a tulip market. Besides the beginning ('When I was only sixteen') the second quatrain of the second verse was absorbed in the 'Song of Fraternisation', which is substituted in Brecht's amended copy of the 1946 script. This also adds that the Cook was called 'Pipe-Henny' because he never took his pipe out of his mouth when he was on the job.

Some light on the camp prostitute's various ages is cast by her ensuing remark about her failure to run him to earth. In the first typescript it happened 'twenty years ago', in the 1946 and Deutches Theater scripts 'ten years ago', before being reduced to the present 'five' some time between 1949 and 1953.

The chaplain's 'Song of the Hours' is adapted from a seventeenth-century hymn by Michael Weisse. It occurs for the first time in the Deutsches Theater script, where it consists of seven verses only and is sung before the curtain to introduce sub-scene 3b, it was cut before the premiére. In Mother Courage's subsequent speech on corruptibility (p. 35) there is a section which was cut in this script but is of interest for its anticipation of *The Caucasian Chalk Circle*:

I used to know a judge in Franconia who was so out for money, even small sums from poor people, that he was universally regarded as a good man right up into Saxony, and that's some way. People talked about him as if he were a saint, he'd listen to everybody, he was tough about the amount—wouldn't let anyone say they were penniless if they had anything—widow or profiteer, he treated them all alike, all of them had to give.

## 4. [4]

The young soldier was originally complaining about the delay in getting his basic pay. Brecht's amendments to his typescript introduced the idea of a special reward, as well as giving Mother Courage more to say. The song was called 'The Song of Waiting' in this typescript and was amended at every stage, first and foremost by adding the (spoken) parentheses.

5. [5]
See p. 46. The cry 'Pshagreff!'—Polish Psia Krew (blood of a dog)—
near the end was simply 'Stop!' until after the 1949 edition.

6. [6]
This scene appeared in the Moscow monthly *Internationale Literatur*
(then edited by J. R. Becher), No. 12, 1940. Courage's speech beginning 'Let's see your money!' was very much longer there, as also in the
first two scripts. The drunken soldier and his song were additions to
the first typescript; Courage's suggestion that he may have been responsible for the attack on Kattrin being an addition to the 1946
script. In *Internationale Literatur* and prior to the Deutsches Theater
version Kattrin accepts the red shoes at the end of the scene and 'sets
about her work; she has calmed down'.

6a. [7]
See p. 56.

7. [8]
This scene (Eilif's death) is the most heavily amended, partly in order to get the confrontation of the cook and Yvette straight. Originally, on the first typescript, she denounces him as 'That's
Surabaya-Johnny', which prompts Courage to hum the refrain of
the song. Courage previously has a song of her own, following the
chaplain's 'Off war, in other words. Aha!' (p. 61), which she introduces by the lines:

> If the Emperor's on top now, what with King of Sweden being dead,
> all it'll mean is that taxes go to the Emperor. Ever seen a water
> wheel? Mills have them. I'm going to sing you a song about one of
> them water wheels, a parable featuring the great. (*She sings the Song
> of the Water Wheel*)

—a song to Eisler's music which is to be found in Brecht's *The Round
Heads and the Pointed Heads*. It was omitted from the 1946 script.

8. [9]
The fourth (St. Martin) verse of the 'Solomon Song' (itself of course
partly taken over from *The Threepenny Opera*) made its appearance in
the 1946 script. The cook's tavern was originally in Uppsala, amended
when he became a Dutchman.

8a. [*10*]
The scene was originally un-numbered. The title was added between
the 1949 and 1953 *Versuche* editions.

9. [*11*]
The date of the title was at first March 1635 and the threatened town
Havelberg. The only change of any substance took place after the
peasant's 'Suppose we got one of the trunks and poked her off . . .',
where in all three scripts the soldiers proceeded to fetch one and actually tried to dislodge Kattrin with it. This was deleted on Brecht's
Deutsches Theater script, which incidentally bears marks showing
exactly where the drumbeats should fall.

9a. [*12*]
See p. 62. On the first typescript lines 5–7 of the song originally read

> He gets his uniform and rations
> The regiment gives him his pay.
> The rest defeats our comprehension
> Tomorrow is another day.

before Brecht amended them to read as now.

### The Threepenny Opera

Brutal, scandalous, perverted, yet humorous, hummable, and with a happy ending, Bertolt Brecht's revolutionary masterpiece is a landmark of modern drama that has become embedded in the Western cultural imagination. Through the love story of Polly Peachum and "Mac the Knife" Macheath, the play satirizes the bourgeois of the Weimar Republic, revealing a society at the height of decadence and on the verge of chaos.  *ISBN 978-0-14-310516-9*

### Mother Courage and Her Children

This chronicle play of the Thirty Years' War was Brecht's response to the ongoing horror of World War II. Following Mother Courage as she trails the armies across Europe, selling provisions from her canteen wagon while her children are devoured by violence, *Mother Courage and Her Children* is nothing less than a classic in the repertory of Western theater.  *ISBN 978-0-14-310528-2*

## Coming from Penguin Classics in Summer 2008

### The Good Person of Szechwan

This remarkable play is one of Bertolt Brecht's most popular works. When three gods come to earth in search of a thoroughly good person, they encounter Sheh Teh, a good-hearted but penniless prostitute, who offers them shelter. Rewarded with enough money to open a tobacco shop "Angel of the Slums" Sheh Teh soon becomes so overwhelmed by the demands of the people seeking assistance that she invents a male alter ego, "Tobacco King" Shui Tah, to ruthlessly deal with the business of living in an evil world. *The Good Person of Szechwan* is a masterpiece of minimalist design and elegance that considers the fundamental qualities of human nature and social mores.  *ISBN 978 0 14-310537-4*

### Life of Galileo

Ranking alongside Mother Courage and Mr. Puntila, Galileo is one of Brecht's most immensely alive, human, and complex characters. In *Life of Galileo*, the great Renaissance scientist is in a brutal struggle for freedom from authoritarian dogma. Unable to resist his appetite for scientific investigation, he comes into conflict with the Inquisition and must publicly adjure his theories, though in private he goes on working on his revolutionary ideas.  *ISBN 978-0-14-310538-1*

# THE STORY OF PENGUIN CLASSICS

**Before 1946** . . . "Classics" are mainly the domain of academics and students; readable editions for everyone else are almost unheard of. This all changes when a little-known classicist, E. V. Rieu, presents Penguin founder Allen Lane with the translation of Homer's *Odyssey* that he has been working on in his spare time.

**1946** Penguin Classics debuts with *The Odyssey*, which promptly sells three million copies. Suddenly, classics are no longer for the privileged few.

**1950s** Rieu, now series editor, turns to professional writers for the best modern, readable translations, including Dorothy L. Sayers's *Inferno* and Robert Graves's unexpurgated *Twelve Caesars*.

**1960s** The Classics are given the distinctive black covers that have remained a constant throughout the life of the series. Rieu retires in 1964, hailing the Penguin Classics list as "the greatest educative force of the twentieth century."

**1970s** A new generation of translators swells the Penguin Classics ranks, introducing readers of English to classics of world literature from more than twenty languages. The list grows to encompass more history, philosophy, science, religion, and politics.

**1980s** The Penguin American Library launches with titles such as *Uncle Tom's Cabin*, and joins forces with Penguin Classics to provide the most comprehensive library of world literature available from any paperback publisher.

**1990s** The launch of Penguin Audiobooks brings the classics to a listening audience for the first time, and in 1999 the worldwide launch of the Penguin Classics website extends their reach to the global online community.

**The 21st Century** Penguin Classics are completely redesigned for the first time in nearly twenty years. This world-famous series now consists of more than 1300 titles, making the widest range of the best books ever written available to millions—and constantly redefining what makes a "classic."

The Odyssey continues . . .

*The best books ever written*

PENGUIN CLASSICS

SINCE 1946

Find out more at www.penguinclassics.com

Visit www.vpbookclub.com